THREE WEEKS
TO BETTER KIDS:

Making Rules that Stick, and
Discipline with a Smile

by George J. Downing, M.Ed.

OmniPress

Sewell, New Jersey

THREE WEEKS TO BETTER KIDS:
Making Rules that Stick, and
Discipline with a Smile

By George J. Downing, M.Ed.

Published by:

OmniPress, Post Office Box 21, Sewell, New Jersey 08080

OmniPress Books may be purchased in quantity for educational, business, or social service use. For information write Special Markets Department, OmniPress, Box 21, Sewell, NJ 08080, or call area code 1-(609) 468-2272 or 1-(800) 507-2272..08.

Cover Design: Jay Summerhill

Library of Congress Catalog Card Number: 96-69937

Downing, George J.

3 Weeks to Better Kids / George J. Downing.—1st OmniPress ed.

ISBN 1-889565-7 : $19.95

Parenting

Child rearing

Family

Classroom management

School discipline

---

96 97 98 99   10 9 8 7 6 5 4 3 2 1

ACKNOWLEDGEMENTS

The psychological roots of Part One of this book, "Making Rules that Stick," can be traced to the pioneering work of Judith Smith and Donald Smith of the University of Michigan at Ann Arbor, with an added dose of the theories of Abraham Herbert Maslow. Part Two, "Discipline with a Smile," goes back to B.F. Skinner's classic work in behavior modification.

Many hundreds of students over twenty-five years have helped to fine-tune the procedures outlined here, and to them we can all be grateful. Others helped proofread for clarity and typos. All have been most encouraging.

Constance Ditzil and Steve Koch have gone the extra mile. My thanks to them. John Henzy, Jesse Wood and Carol Hupping were especially supportive.

But the human touch—the love and humor which has emerged in this effort—originates from the warm and stimulating relationships I have enjoyed with my wife, Sherry, and our children, Tom, Melissa, Laurie, Jerry, Cindy, Richard, and Beth, and their fine spouses and children.

Some scholars may be appalled at the vernacular tone. I must accept the blame for all such audacity and any errors myself. My intent was to keep the book practical and readable.

iii

Table of Contents

PART TWO: Discipline with a Smile

Preface

There are at least two ways to write a book about children's behavior. One is the scholarly approach, citing all the available evidence from countless experiments. A second is the experiential approach, using practical observations from real life by ordinary people.

I'd like to think of myself as a scholar, and if I'd written for my peers in education or psychology this book would be in quite a different form. But I've chosen to write as a teacher, a mentor, a friend, offering some relief to harried parents who need techniques that will work immediately.

This book, then, is a hands-on, practical approach filled with anecdotes and simple methods that you can use. It was written at the urging of my students who have applied these ideas and found them so useful they wanted something they could share with their families and friends. I have had hundreds of students—who also happened to be parents—report rewarding stories of their lives being greatly improved by these things which I now pass on to you.

My peers, unless they are also stressed-out parents, would probably have preferred the scholarly approach. But when you're being tyrannized by a child in your own home or classroom, who you gonna call—Statisticians or Bratbusters?

Good morning, this is Bratbusters. We may write in an authoritarian mode and we may sound irreverent and even audacious. But we think you'll stay awake, and we honestly believe 85% of those who try these techniques will be so pleased they'll push copies of the book at every suffering parent they know.

I hope you're among those who find relief, and I'd like to hear about your successes or modifications you've made that work for you. Since I live three other lives, I may not be able to respond to everything you might write, but if you'll write, I'll read. You can always get through to me at OmniPress, Box 21, Sewell, NJ 08080, or if your local paper carries "Dear Old Dad," write me there.

Live well and prosper, and may you have reasonable children in a mild, pleasant, loving home.

IMPROVING CHILDREN'S BEHAVIOR

Part One: MAKING RULES THAT STICK

Chapter 1— An Introduction
Will this really work?

I enjoy children. Some of them I love, some I tolerate, and some I just look at and mutter, "I'd like to have that kid for three weeks."

Three weeks is all it takes, maximum—usually much less. The truth is, and I'm reluctant to say this because you probably won't believe me, I have seen many miserably difficult kids turned around overnight. 180 degrees. It may happen for you overnight. Or you might have to be patient and wait for three weeks—no more—before things around your home will be much better.

I worked in the public schools for ten years and loved it. Friends would say, "I could never be a schoolteacher. I couldn't stand the hassle." *I* never had any hassle. Well. . . after the first three weeks of the school year, after I'd gotten them shaped up, I never—or very rarely—had a hassle. I loved my students, and I think most of the kids felt the same about me.

My students were in their seats when the bell rang. They were relaxed, with lots of good will and humor, but no one talked while I was talking. They stayed in their seats after the dismissal bell until *I* dismissed them. When there was an assembly and the administration insisted that classes march from their rooms to the auditorium in silence, my class was the only really silent group. Notice: silent, not sullen.

What strange power did I have over these children? Was it mass hypnotism? Dire threats? No. It's nothing you couldn't do if you were to follow the simple, basic ideas in this book.

I remember being one of four teachers assigned to proctor a study hall. I don't think I ever shouted at a student, humiliated him, or was anything but courteous. But after three weeks, there was absolutely no talking, and my collegues would beg off to go for coffee or to their rooms for preparation, leaving me happily alone with 203 silent kids while I graded papers.

I'd be in the public schools yet, except that a community college was built near my home and I was invited to be on the faculty. I've been teaching child psychology (among other things) there for over twenty-five years, and have had the pleasure of helping hundreds of non-traditional students (i.e., parents) get their own kids in order.

I've been a scoutmaster and an advisor to youth organizations. I've taken groups of over a hundred on walking tours of Philadelphia and Washington, to camps and conferences, museums and gardens. It takes some preparation to get them ready, but once they're squared away, it's a great experience for all.

At home, my good wife and I waited anxiously for six years for our first child and finished nine years later with our seventh. Seven kids in a three-bedroom home!

We had them stacked into triple bunks in one room, in two double-deck bunks in a larger room, and the parents in the tiny third bedroom.

They say if you can manage three kids you can manage any number. I believe it, because the principles for managing even one without losing your mind are the same as managing a whole tribe. I'm going to teach you those principles, and the quality of your life is going to improve dramatically.

As our children got older we divided the old master bedroom with a new wall and gave a couple of daughters some privacy. One of the boys decided he wanted to train to be an arctic explorer, and so we built a loft in the attic of the unheated attached garage for him. (He actually worked in Greenland seven years later.) Another had a cold bedroom partitioned from part of the same garage. It was a full house.

In some games a full house is a winning hand, and so it was with us. My memories of that time in our lives are very pleasant. The children weren't perfect, but I guess I'm not, either. And they didn't always make the decisions I would have liked them to make, but they might say the same thing about me. In the important things, they were just fine.

We had a crowded and hectic home, but a mild and loving one. There were lots of games, singing, and reading. They were not allowed to say mean things to their mother, and I tolerated no more hassles at home than I did in the classroom. Oh, there was some subtle one-up-man-ship going on between the brothers and sisters, but arguing and fighting were nipped in the bud.

How did this happen? What was I, some kind of latter-day pied piper? Did I resort to clever oriental techniques of brainwashing? Or did I study *Mein Kampf* nightly ("We have ways of making you. . .)?

None of the above. I used simple ideas which you can learn quickly. They work. My experience has shown that about 85% of those who try them succeed beyond their dreams. About 5% fail because they change a crucial part and the results don't follow. Another 5% have kids with whom these techniques just don't work. (Or, it may be there are some subtleties we haven't been able to identify which prevent them from working.) The last 5% perversely enjoy being martyred by their kids and so they unconsciously sabotage their own efforts. (This isn't a copout on my part. For many people, suffering is their claim to fame.)

I'm going to show you two powerful techniques which will change your kids into pleasant, reasonable, obedient children, and do it fast. The first technique I call, "Making Rules that Stick." It's very basic and predictable. The second is like icing on the cake and I'd recommend you use it *after* you get the first one in place. I call it "Discipline with a Smile," and it makes raising kids fun. The kids, especially, love it, and I'll show you all of the pitfalls we've learned in twenty-five years so that you can avoid them.

Does this really work? Yes, it does, for I've seen it and done it. Will it work for you? It has for hundreds of my students, and I believe you can make it work, too.

Chapter 2— A Rationale For Having Obedient Children:

Parents Who are Verbally and Emotionally Abused

We hear a lot about child abuse these days. I'm against it. But I'm also against abuse of parents by their children. I'm not talking about "elderly abuse." I'm talking about ordinary parents in their twenties, thirties, or forties who are berated and humiliated by their own children.

I don't ask that children speak only when spoken to nor that they answer "Yes, sir" and "Yes ma'm." (The latter make a good impression when you hear them, though.) But I do believe that children need to be courteous when they speak to anyone, especially to their parents.

Our culture has it backwards. Have you ever wondered why most children can be the pinnacle of good manners when speaking to a stranger, a bit too familiar when talking with a neighbor, perhaps a little cheeky to their grandparents, and absolutely rude to their own mothers and fathers? If anyone is to be short changed on manners, why should it be parents?

Case Studies

If the above sounds like your house, you are not alone. There are millions of parents who despair of ever having any peace until the last of their children leaves home. I know a man who says he gives his children the same gift for their eighteenth birthday: a suitcase, with the comment that they need to use it before they're nineteen.

"Dear Abby" recently had a grandmother write complaining that she had eight grandchildren, only three of whom she could stand for more than thirty minutes. The other five were "ill-mannered, rude, demanding whiners—all under the age of nine." I wish this book had been in print at the time. I would have forwarded a copy to her with my sympathy.

You've seen the same thing all around you. I'll wager each of the following situations sounds familiar. I've changed the names and massaged the situations slightly to protect their privacy, but for every one described here, you can believe there are plenty of parents who will think I've been following them around taking notes.

Allison

Allison was in the profession of her dreams. Even as a child she loved beautiful things. She was a born romantic, and when other teens were pouring over movie and rock magazines, she was clipping furniture ads and planning a twentieth century *Tara*. Oh, for the days of hoop skirts, balconies, and pink roses on the wallpaper!

In college she studied art and aesthetics. She graduated with a major in interior design and went to work for a small but prestigeous decorating firm in New York. Barry was her liaison to a brokerage house who had contracted her firm to design the offices for their new location. One thing led to another until they decided to use her talents to decorate their own home.

While their children were in infancy and toddlerhood, Allison kept her hand in as a consultant, and now she had her own business. The word was out that she was the designer of choice if you wanted someone who could read your mind and express it in exciting but exquisite taste.

The children were in school now, and they had their friends and their own interests which occupied them before dinnertime.

It was dinner that was the problem. Or rather, that's when the problems began. Cecily was never there on time, and David wouldn't eat. It was call and shout and scream, plead, cajole, and threaten. By the end of the meal Allison was wound up like a spring, Barry was eating in stony silence, and the children were complaining and insulting her in ways she never would have dreamed of doing when she was a child.

The evening was little better. Was the homework done? When would the room be cleaned? No, you can't watch that program. And, please, please, turn that music down!

Bedtime was 8:30 for the children. Or, that was the time for the nightly struggle to get them into bed. Arguments, excuses, dawdling, and just plain obstructionism were the agenda, until when the children were finally down, it was near 10:00, Allison was exhausted and Barry exasperated.

As she collapses with a sigh in the living room, she asks herself, "How can a woman who makes top dollar in a respected position be tyrannized by children who haven't even gone through puberty?"

Ed

Ed's story was just a variation of Allison's. He was a regional manager for a medical supply house, and if you added up all the sales reps, warehouse workers and temps, he had about a hundred people to do his bidding. Secretaries sat up straight when he walked in and they called him "sir." Foremen and group leaders tried to demonstrate their loyalty, and even his superiors were appreciative of his ideas.

His wife, Fran, was a pleasant sort. She had her own ways, certainly, but she loved him and that was important.

Greg was Ed's problem. Greg was fourteen, and he had been getting more and more difficult each year. Ed had always thought that he and his son would grow together as buds—pals. They would camp together and build doghouses together and be friends. But that's not how it had turned out.

Everything Ed thought would be fun, Greg thought was stupid. It had started early, when Greg preferred sitting for endless hours wiggling a joy-stick at jagged figures on the TV screen. He was one of the "in" crowd, and he advised his father on what things weren't cool. Soon, all of Ed's interests evoked sighs and rollings of the eyeballs from his son.

More recently had come the sullen silence and frightening styles of dress and grooming. The biweekly blowups were becoming more frequent, with both Ed and Greg shouting things deliberately designed to hurt the other.

Harry, one of Ed's close associates was divorced. He'd moved into a small apartment of his own, had quiet meals by himself or ate out, and watched the TV shows of his choice or turned up his fifteen hundred dollar quadraphonic sound system. He enjoyed the latest Tom Clancy novels and flew occasionally just to see a ball game.

Ed loved Fran and he supposed he loved Greg, but during the tough times at home he found thoughts of Harry's self-controlled life flickering around the edges of his consciousness, and it worried him.

Ed wondered, "How can a man who commands the attention of a hundred employees be so completely dismissed by his own son?"

Ilene

Ilene spent a lot of energy pleasing others. As a child she was her mother's right arm, watching the babies and changing their diapers, and even learning to cook at a young age in order to help out before her mother got home from work. She liked being depended upon.

In high school she attracted the attention of a general loser named Jack. Nobody understood him, but she nurtured him and was able to persuade him to stay in school.

After graduation (now that they were adults, of course), there seemed to be no reason why they shouldn't get married. Her mother didn't like him, but Ilene was sure that with the help of a good woman Jack would settle down and straighten out.

When he would lose his temper on the job and get fired, Ilene's paycheck kept them afloat. When he started drinking more heavily and some nights not even coming home, she knew things weren't right with their marriage. Perhaps he would become more responsible after the baby was born.

It didn't happen. He had slapped her around a couple of times while they were going together, but now he became outright abusive. Ilene endured for the sake of their son, Kenny.

When the child was three, Jack was a total waste. He was into drugs, had been jailed briefly twice, and the drunken beatings had become routine. Ilene decided the pattern wasn't going to change and she pulled the plug.

She talked to her nineteen-year-old brother, Luke, and persuaded him to go in with her on a garden apartment. She worked at the hospital from 11:00 at night until 7:00 in the morning. She'd come home and get Kenny ready for school and then sleep during the day. She was always there when the boy got home, and then she'd make dinner for them and Luke. Luke's only obligation was his share of the rent and to be home before she left for work at night. It seemed like an ideal arrangement.

Except for Kenny. Kenny was not an easy child. He really needed a strong hand, a father. But *she* didn't need a husband like Jack, and unfortunately, Luke wasn't much of a father image. About the best he could muster was directed at her. "You really shouldn't take that from him, Ilene. He's going to grow up to be a real handful."

Kenny was a handful now, but in her words, "I've already deprived him of his father, and I just can't bring myself to discipline him. I feel guilty enough." Dumb, dumb, but that's how she felt.

Ilene reached the breaking point in the middle of October, the year Kenny started kindergarten. She began getting notes from his teacher.

"Kenny needs to practice his social skills. Please help him understand about waiting his turn and not talking when others are talking."

The notes got stronger. "Kenny is socially immature, and perhaps you should consider withdrawing him until next year."

The humiliating climax came one afternoon when
Ilene was sitting in her living room watching a program
and waiting for Kenny to get home. Suddenly the door
burst open and Kenny rushed in, ran across the room
into his bedroom and slammed the door. About ten feet
behind him was the school bus driver, who braked
himself just inside the front door.

"I'm sorry, lady, I didn't mean to come in your
house, but I don't have to take that stuff! You've got to
do something about that kid! I don't have to drive kids
like that." Backing out slowly, he repeated, "Look, I'm
sorry about stepping into your house, but you've got to
straighten him out if he's going to ride *my* bus."

After the tears of humiliation and embarrassment,
Ilene was ready for a ten-week community course called,
"Improving Your Child's Behavior." That's where we
met.

She came with a woman from a neighboring
apartment. I remember thinking of the woman as "Tug-
Boat Annie," though that, of course, wasn't her name.
More about Annie and her profane and promiscuous
thirteen-year-old daughter later.

Chapter 3— Help Is On The Way:
Behavior Can Be Changed

I'm here to say that parents don't have to put up with this kind of nonsense. I'm here to say that our children came to live with us, not us with them, and *they're* going to have to do some adjusting, too. You had a home before they got here and you'll have a home eighteen years later when they leave. Meantime, they're guests in your home.

It *is* your home. You chose the curtains and the dishes, and you didn't feel it necessary to get an eight-place setting of Flintstone china because you had to please the kids.

Nor should you feel it necessary to endure endless hours of hyperactive turtles on your TV, nor 130 decibels of monotone rap urging the dusting of the nation's police. It's yooour home.

"I know they're the most popular group on MTV, dear. Why don't you write down the names of your favorite songs so that when you have your own home you can listen to them all day?" Try to say this with a straight face, without bombast or cynicism, if you can. He'll sense you're pulling his leg, but not be quite sure. Gives you a bit of an edge.

Or try, "Yes, dear. When you get married you can have vending machines in your kitchen and your family won't have to sit down together at the table at all. They can eat whenever they please. But in the meantime, this is the way we do it *here*."

Of course, you don't want to carry this to its illogical extreme. The kids do live here, too, and this is their home, for a while, at least. The point is, rank has its privilege, and when final decisions are made, the call is rightfully yours.

In fact, that's really what a lot of the hassle is about: who makes the decision? It's less about what TV program is on, or when bedtime is, than it is about power.

I'm here to tell you that you have the legitimate right to power in your home, and if you've lost it, I want to show you how you can get it back and use it wisely. And more than that, I'll show you that your children really want it that way.

Remember Ilene and Kenny? Before she finished my ten-week, one-hour-per-week course in "Improving Your Child's Behavior," she brought in a note from Kenny's teacher. I wish I'd had the wits to ask her to let me keep it, but the truth is she was so proud of it she probably framed it. The best I can remember, it read something like, "I believe in giving credit where credit's due. I don't know what you've done with Kenny, but he's a changed boy. All the children like him and he's one of my favorite students."

I couldn't resist milking that for all I could get, so I asked Ilene, "That's amazing. A few weeks ago he was a terror to everybody, and now he's a joy at school and at home. To what do you attribute this reversal?"

The others in the class knew I was pushing it and they laughed, but Ilene played the role.

She grinned and said, "It was the rule."

Let me tell you how all this happened. Let me show you how to make rules that stick, and how this can have an impact far beyond just having beds made or dogs fed or trash carried out. It will change your kids for the better and make your own life satisfying.

First we need to lay some groundwork on what motivates people in general and children in particular. It will help us to understand why they *want* rules.

Chapter 4— Some Background:
A Hierarchy Of Needs

    Abraham Herbert Maslow believed he could rank people's motives, and that everyone has the same ranking, or hierarchy, of motives. He worked on his theories until his early death a few years ago, and what you understand of Maslow depends on when he wrote what you read. Still, I believe he would approve of the following.

    Some texts show Maslow's Hierarchy of Needs as a pyramid. For me, a set of stair steps works better to convey the idea that you have to master one step before being able to concentrate on another.

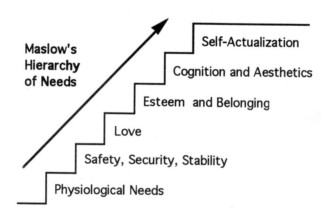

**Maslow's
Hierarchy
of Needs**

Self-Actualization

Cognition and Aesthetics

Esteem and Belonging

Love

Safety, Security, Stability

Physiological Needs

Of course, we work on all of these needs, but we really can't focus on higher ones until we get the lower ones under control. Let's look at each of them.

PHYSIOLOGICAL NEEDS

Maslow believed that our physical needs are the most important. That is, we are greatly concerned about getting enough air, enough water, enough food and warmth, to be in good health, etc. Until these needs are satisfied, other needs are secondary.

I know, John Lennon said, "Love is All You Need," but for Maslow, though you may think about love, survival is where it's at.

Marooned on a desert island, only a hundred yards' swim from a paradise of running streams and coconuts, you will stay with the safety of the island only until your thirst—your physiological need—drives you to risk that safety.

Forced into the Warsaw Ghetto, you will be afraid of the Nazi machine guns only until hunger urges you to crawl through the sewer tunnels to search for food on the outside.

Your love of beauty will send you across the world collecting art, until those nagging chest pains turn your attention to your physiological needs, and color, light and shadow pale into insignificance. Art comes after heart.

Some people call it simply the survival instinct. We'll call it physiological needs—the first and most important step on Maslow's Hierarchy of Needs.

SAFETY, SECURITY,
AND STABILITY NEEDS

Safety, security, and stability are all one and the same, but just on different levels of abstraction.

Maslow thought that after you were comfortable with your physiological needs, then your interest focused on safety, security, and stability. Oh, yes, you still go grocery shopping so you can eat and you buy winter coats to keep warm, but these things become secondary because they have been satisfied. And, yes, you still want to love and be loved, but that doesn't dominate your thinking until safety, security and stability is under control.

Safety is terribly important. The country mouse packs up and leaves the gourmet life of his city cousin when he learns about the cat. Your own quality of life drops to intolerable levels when there are muggings and burglaries on your block.

We need *security*, a kind of long-range safety. We stay at the hated job because it's steady, secure. We suffer with the known devil rather than risk the unknown one. We haven't talked to Dad since Fathers' Day, but his sudden death wipes us out because he was a symbol of security to us.

Stability is just more of the same, but broader. We need predictability in our lives. We need to know where the next paycheck is coming from. We need to know that the train/bus/plane will be on time. We're irritated that the O.J. trial has pre-empted the regular afternoon programming, even if we don't watch afternoon TV. It bothers us when our spouse changes hair style or rearranges the furniture, not because the new is worse, but because it's different.

Maslow says safety, security, and stability is more important than love. The romantic protests, "But, ah, what I did for love!" Was it really love? Or was it the physiological need for, well, something else? Perhaps it was a need to be validated as a person, which is a safety, security, and stability problem after all.

I'll wager you have a friend who, though in love with the playboy or debutante, married the accountant. Maybe it was you.

"What is this world coming to?" we mutter. "It wasn't like this when I was a kid." Some cynic suggests it's just as well we die after three score years and ten, because we couldn't take much more of the changes we're seeing.

Safety, security, and stability—almost as important as survival, the physiological needs.

LOVE NEEDS

Ah, yes, we do need love. We need somebody to love and we need love from somebody. We will deny our own preferences and sacrifice our own pleasures to insure that we are loved.

Melanie's home is affluent and efficient. Her parents have provided for her every need, almost. But she doesn't feel loved. "Oh," they protest, "we work very hard to give her whatever she wants. There are a lot of kids who would give their right arms to have the things she has.''

But she doesn't feel loved. She's got food, clothes, a comfortable home, and her life is stable and predictable. But she doesn't feel the warmth of human kindness that flows from spontaneous love.

Spike Lee titled his film, "She's Gotta Have It." But it's love she's got to have, and that's sometimes confused with sex. And she will get it. She'll look for it from some boy who will swear his undying love for her, and then demand that she "prove her love for him" by doing things that will put her at serious risk.

(I've never understood why this line works. Why shouldn't he prove *his* love for *her* by protecting her from the dangers of early sex. The line does work, though. It worked last night somewhere in the world, it will work tonight, and your grandchildren will hear it when they come of age.)

I remember attending the retirement dinner for an elementary school teacher who had spent her entire career in the same school district. During the evening some insensitive oaf commented to her, "Miss Nelson, it's too bad you never had any children. You would have been a wonderful mother."

Listen to her revealing reply, accompanied by a deceptively sweet smile and piercing eye. "Oh, but you're wrong. I've had hundreds of children."

I suppose that's much to be preferred over the solution of the old lady down the street who has twenty-six cats, all with names and personalities.

Seriously, though, I've known lonely people whose pets were like children, on whom they lavished love and received it in return. There's even serious thought these days about providing pets in nursing homes, where they can help to meet the love needs of the lonely and forgotten.

Pets. They're called pets because we like to pet them. We spend hard earned cash to support them because we need their love and to love them. (Does that make pets prostitutes? Argh! Try that one on your philosopher friend.)

To sum it up: after physiological needs and safety/security/ stabililty needs, we must have love, one way or another.

ESTEEM NEEDS

For Maslow, we all have the need to be well thought of, esteemed, but this is not as important as the need to be loved.

You can remember that poor girl in your high school who bought assurance that she was loved by sleeping with that creepy senior. Her friends protested, "Don't you know what people are saying?" She didn't care what people were saying or thinking. She needed love first before esteem.

It's nice to drive a prestigeous car and live in the right neighborhood. It's nice to have the money to wear the latest styles and imitate the beautiful people. For some, becoming employee of the month is intensely satisfying. But they would trade it all to feel deeply and truly loved.

Esteem needs are there, but they are pale until our physiological, safety/security/stability, and love needs are met.

Now, it's easy to misunderstand what is happening here. You can probably think of people whose love needs are in shambles but who spend a great deal of time and energy on what others think. If that's all there were to it, Maslow's theories would fall with the passing of a butterfly.

But try asking, are such people really worried about esteem, or are they worried about their place in society, their niche? If this is the case, they're probably really working on safety/security/stability and not necessarily on esteem needs.

Do they dress to be appreciated, or do they dress for success to be seen as part of the safe "in" crowd, where they'll be tapped for promotions in a secure career?

The fourth grader who won't wear the yellow raincoat this year and the teenager who pierces her eyebrow with miniature barbells may be working on esteem. And they'll sacrifice their parents' love over the issue because they're also working on being safely and securely a part of their group. (The mother who asks, "Well, who's more important: your parents or your friends?" has asked the wrong question.)

Do actors argue over the size of their names on the credits because they need esteem, or because they need to defend and enhance their position in a precarious and fickle showbusiness? Or maybe it's that "Oh, My Papa" will be proud and love me if I'm a famous success.

What often looks like esteem needs is really something much more basic.

AESTHETIC AND COGNITION NEEDS

After all these other needs are satisfied, Maslow believes we start to focus on beauty and knowledge, i.e., aesthetics and cognition.

The newlyweds can be happy in a one-bedroom basement apartment with orange crates for bureaus, but in later life, with their needs for security, love, and esteem met, they get rid of the second-hand stuff and buy the new home with the skylights and wall-to-wall carpeting.

The wife who is comfortable with her situation then begins to crave the college degree she abandoned for love. It's not because she wants the possible job security from the degree, nor does she want the prestige. She just wants to learn. Professors often find these non-traditional students to be lights in the forest, high points in their day.

But what happens when the husband who has been driving hours every weekend to visit antique shows comes home to find his wife packing? While he's been gone satisfying his aesthetic needs, her love needs have been met by the local Lothario.

"Please, honey, come back! I love you!"

"Not enough," she says. "Go make love to your parson's bench."

"I don't care about the antiques. I can't live without you," he complains.

Notice he has lost interest in aesthetics because more basic needs are threatened. It may indeed be that he needs her *love*. But it may also be that he needs the *stability* she provides in his home, or even the *esteem* of his friends. What will they think of him when they hear he's been cuckolded? What a complex bundle we are! How does anyone ever make it through life?

SELF-ACTUALIZATION NEEDS

When a person has met all of the earlier basic needs, he emerges as a "self-actualized personality," with fifteen to twenty very nice characteristics. But that's another story, and our concern here is children and their needs. It's not likely that any child is going to have all of his/her hierarchy of needs met and emerge as a self-actualizer.

THE CHILD AND THE HIERARCHY OF NEEDS

While an adult may become a self-actualizer after a few years (most do not), children are stuck working near the bottom of the ladder.

Can a child meet his physiological needs? Yes, if he's getting enough to eat, he's warm, and is generally healthy.

How about safety, security, and stability? Probably not. This is the sticking point for children. The world was not built for their comfort. It is a fearsome and dangerous place.

There are the playground bullies. Every generation has its bullies. "Want to have a near-death experience, Twinkie?" asks Calvin's nemesis. (But have you noticed *you* never got to be one of the big kids? Strange.)

It may be less personal. In my high school we practiced nuclear holocaust with air raid drills, during which we sat on the floor in the basement corridor and put our heads between our knees to protect them from glass bursting in from the expected blast. This was the "Happy Days" decade?

My own children had Mother Earth-type teachers who just about traumatized them over pollution. "The establishment will get you if you don't watch out."

Today's children are warned about someone using a "bad touch" on them; maybe someone in their own family—an uncle, or grandfather, or even their own father.

"Come sit on my lap, honey, and tell me about your day."

"Ummm, ummm, nothing," with finger in mouth, worried wrinkles on forehead, and body rigid. Was that a "bad touch" just then?

They're told about strangers luring them into cars. The milk cartons in their lunchrooms show pictures of the unfortunates: "Have you seen this child?"

From their earliest years there have been monsters under their beds, ugly shadows projected on their darkened ceilings from the streetlight, and bad dreams they can't distinguish from reality.

Add to this an angry parent twice their height and three times their weight who someday might really lose it and do them in. "If I catch you doing that again I'll cut it off!"

Security? What about the teachers who teach one thing and test another? Or being dropped from the team? Or left back to repeat a grade? Or being abandoned to a harsh and sadistic baby-sitter or day-care provider?

Stability? "Now that you're in fourth grade, dear, you get to take the school bus to Edge-of-the-Earth Elementary School." Or, "Guess what? Daddy's got a promotion, and we're going to move to a new state, where you'll be able to meet lots of new friends."

No, it's a rare child who is able to meet his safety, security, and stability needs.

And, yet, he really can't progress to enjoy love, esteem, beauty, and knowledge unless he gets those basic needs under control.

THE PARENTS' ROLE

What can a parent do to help meet the child's safety, security, and stability needs? Should he turn down promotions, walk the kid to and from school, give him a nightlight, or build a family bed?

No need. That's what this book is all about. There are ways to fill his safety, security, and stability needs sufficiently so that the child can weather many of the affronts to him and become free to move on to bigger things. And it's not as hard as you might think. It's not hard at all, and it has some wonderful side effects for everyone. It just takes a little forethought.

Chapter 5— Consistency:
The Key To Security

In generations past, even if there were threats of a sort, the world provided many things a child could depend on. But a lot of these are gone today.

There was seed time and harvest. By the time he was ten, he had seen and could predict the rhythm of the earth. But in the U.S. of today, only three per cent of the population are tied to the patterns of the farm, and only half of that if you factor out the conglomerates of agribusiness and just count family farms.

No, for most of us the seasons are very secondary to our lives, dictating only whether we wear long sleeves or short sleeves. Our homes, offices and schools are largely climate controlled: 72° year round, and we're hardly aware of the weather. "Red sky at morning, sailors take warning. Red sky at night, sailors' delight." Huh? Whuzzat mean?

Even night and day have little meaning. Years ago, when the sun went down we might read a bit by the fireside, but generally night time meant bedtime, and we rose with the sun. No more. We're often surprised to go outside and find it dark already, so we switch on the headlights and shop in the brightly lit malls and watch the late TV show until we're good and ready for sleep.

My little home town had "blue laws," which required that businesses close on Sunday. Everyone knew about it and could predict their schedules on a seven-day cycle. We wore special clothes that day and ate dinner at a different time. Today, one day runs into another. There is no predictable pattern. Fifteen more shopping days 'til Christmas means fifteen more calendar days, all very much the same.

THE FATE OF THE UNRULY

Among other things, children who don't know how to obey rules are unpopular. From sandbox to prom night, classroom to summer camp, they become legends in their own time. Others may laugh at them, or let them walk as pointmen to see what rules will be enforced, but they're really not accepted.

Many rules are reasonable and they make life work smoothly. But the kid who is splashing and dunking everyone disrupts the swimming lesson, and the others go home disgruntled because he prevented the instructor from doing as much with them.

"Don't invite Rudy the Wrecker! He'll blow out the candles before the birthday boy, and later throw icing and get cake on the carpet."

Unfortunately, Rudy's unpopularity will cause him anger and resentment, leading to more aggressive behavior, a false front for his insecurity.

Even adult rule breakers are ostracized. Who wants to sit near someone in a theater who has to comment on every line? Who wants to invite the habitual late comer to a dinner party, or the drunk who gets sick in your bathroom? Most social rules are outgrowths of simple courtesy, the oil that lubricates the wheels of civilization. Ignore them and you become abrasive.

The world doesn't trust you if it can't predict your behavior. John Molloy of *Dress for Success* tells of a man who almost missed a promotion because he showed up at a dinner party wearing a red vest under his jacket. This is unfair, but it happened. The unspoken suspicion was, "What else might he do that we can't predict?" There was a happy ending, however, when someone learned that his teenager had given him the vest for Christmas and the father wore it one night to show he appreciated the thought. What a relief! He's one of us, one of the old boys, after all.

USING RULES AS TOOLS

Where will children get the comfort and security that came from predictable times, seasons, and sabbaths? One answer is in rules. We can use "rules as tools"— rules designed to give them safety, security and stability, rules that they can depend upon. Children *want* things they can predict and depend upon.

Think back for a minute to your high school years. Do you remember the time you were supposed to be home by midnight and you came in at 12:05? Your father was standing at the top of the stairs and chewed on you for being irresponsible and undependable, immature and willing to put your parents through anguish because of your thoughtlessness, and you're grounded for three weeks!

"Whew," you thought, "I've got to shape up." So you endured the three weeks and finally were released back into the land of the living. Your first night out, the cycle broke down on the way back, and you and your date huddled under an overpass in the rain until a police car came by and took you to the next town. Another cop took you to the border of your home town, and the locals picked you up there and brought you home.

You crept into the darkened house at 1:30 in the morning. Silence. Up the stairs, quietly, quietly. Near the top a stair step squeeked loudly.

"Is that you, dear?"

"Yea-sss," very meekly.

"Are you all right?"

"Yes, but the bike broke down and we couldn't get to a phone and the police brought us home."

"All right. We're glad you're okay. Good night."

That's it?!! That's all, for an hour and a half overdue? You got crunched for being five minutes late before, now that's all there is? I mean, that's good I guess, but, man, you never know what's happening around this place. I wish they'd get their act together so you'd know what to expect!

Children want rules. But they want good rules, consistently enforced.

Sergeant Bud Hulsey has interviewed thousands of kids during his career in law enforcement. He tells of a sixteen-year-old girl who was as close to a nervous breakdown as anyone he'd ever seen.

Her parents were wealthy, and when she turned sixteen she whined and fussed for a new Trans-Am until they bought her one. Then she argued to stay out until 2:00 AM driving her new Trans-Am until they finally gave in. Then she wanted to cruise around with a bad crowd and she whined and fussed until they threw up their hands and said okay, okay, she could choose her own friends.

Only two things, they said. "First, don't get in trouble with the law, and second, don't get pregnant 'til you get out of high school."

She sat talking with Bud in his office, and with tears streaming down her face she told him, "You know, Mr. Hulsey, my folks don't love me."

Well, I expect they did. What they didn't know is that children are afraid of the world, and in spite of their forays into independence, they expect and want their parents to protect them.

Your fourteen-year-old performs a dramatic scene of tragedy because you won't let her go overnight to some college boy's homecoming weekend. But this may be an obligatory protest and a chance to explore the emotions of rebellion. Deep inside, she's likely grateful for your protection.

Children want rules—good rules. Rules wrap them up in security. Rules help them predict their chaotic world.

Then why don't they accept our rules? There are several reasons, and here are a few:

1. Sometimes we make up poor rules.
2. Sometimes they're exercising their wings of independence, on which they'll have to fly by themselves soon enough.
3. Sometimes they're testing to see if we'll enforce the rule, and they're secretly happy when we do.
4. Sometimes they're so tired of our wimpishness they act absolutely outrageous in an effort to force us to be firm.
5. Sometimes they're putting on an act for their friends so they can lay the blame on us.

Here's a pitiful story for you. Ollie was playing in the sand box with his new truck when his mother called him for dinner. He paid no attention.

Penny said, "Isn't that your mother?"

"Yes, but I don't have to go yet," and he continued playing while his mother's calls became louder.

Then came a voice from another direction. "Penneeee!"

"I've got to go," Penny told him, and she picked up her toys and ran.

Ollie played for a bit longer, until his mother hit seventy-eight decibels and began using his full name. Then he went home, a little sobered and unaccountably just a little jealous of Penny.

That evening while his father was reading the newspaper, Ollie took his new truck to him.

"Daddy, this is my truck, but I want you to have it and if I want to play with it, I'll have to ask you. Okay?"

Ollie's father didn't pick up on what was happening. He had been raised by a hypercritical and harsh father who dictated his every move, and he'd vowed he would never do that to *his* child.

What was going on here? Ollie had no rules. His parents used explanation and persuasion and generally suffered along with his contrariness. He was spoiled and he knew it. He was out of control and he frightened himself. He wanted limits—he wanted rules.

Ollie's dad didn't understand this. "What do you mean?" he countered. "You got that truck for your birthday. It's yours. You can play with it anytime you want."

And Ollie walked away a little sad, wishing he had some rules he had to follow. True story.

RULES FOR CHILDREN

Ollie's father gave him no rules because he loved him and wanted him to have a better childhood than he'd had. There's virtue in that. We don't want our children to fall out of bed at reveille, dress by the numbers, and stand for inspection before marching to the school bus.

But they do need rules. A few rules. The fewer the better, almost. There are several reasons.

One reason is that we need some peace in our own home. We work hard until we're tired, and then we need to relax and become refreshed. We can't do that if our kids are harder to handle than our jobs. Our effectiveness in our careers and the quality of our lives depend upon the atmosphere in our homes. It *is* possible to have a home life that's peaceful, orderly, and even fun, and we're getting to that.

A second reason is that kids who can't follow rules get hassled in school and in the neighborhood. They reject the world's rules and the world rejects them. Feeling rejected they reject the world, and their young lives deteriorate into a vicious cycle of rejection, resentment and rebellion.

Another reason is that the child needs to grow into an adult who can control himself. The Hillside Strangler left notes, "Stop me before I kill more." Compulsive gamblers and wayward spouses haven't learned control and they ruin more lives than their just own.

But few children can control themselves. At birth they're totally egocentric, no altruism whatsoever. You steadied them while they were learning to balance a bicycle, and they have to learn to balance their lives. Someone outside of them must control them, and then as they grow, the adult should ease up and back off, allowing them more and more control of themselves.

Have you ever known a kid who was constantly in trouble, breaking every rule until everyone thought he'd be hanged before he was thirty? Then he went into the military, and when he came home on leave he looked sharp and called everyone "sir" and "m'am." Somebody had controlled him, and now he could transfer that control from them to himself.

We impose control on children so that when they become independent they can impose their own control on themselves. And the earlier the better.

There's yet another reason, and that's why we spent so much time discussing Maslow's Hierarchy of Needs. We use rules as tools to give children safety, security, and stability, so that they can move ahead with their lives and learn love, esteem, beauty, and knowledge, and maybe even some day become self-actualizers.

But we must have good rules, consistently enforced.

Characteristics Of A Good Rule

A number of years ago a team of psychologists—Judith Smith and Donald Smith at Ann Arbor, Michigan, put out a little booklet called "Child Management." I used it in my child psychology classes until it went out of print, and my students found it rather effective.

Smith and Smith urged caregivers to develop rules with three characteristics. Since then, my students and I have added a fourth characteristic which makes the technique even more powerful. Here are the four qualities for a good rule, a rule which will have the impact we've been talking about in the previous pages.

1. DEFINABLE

First, a good rule must be definable. That means the child must know exactly what you expect.

It's not enough to tell him he should do a "good job." What is a "good job?"

"Looks good to me," he says.

"Well, it doesn't look good to me, and you know that's not what I meant!" So you're off to another knock down, drag out hassle over his ability to read minds, and you're really upset, which was his desired effect when he "did" the job in the first place.

"Now you come home soon."

When is "soon"? Within the hour? Before lunch? Today? That's almost as bad as "Do a good job" or "Don't stay out late."

You protest that he really should know what you meant. Well, he probably does, but remember, we're talking about power here, and he will wrest it from you if he can. Children like to play Eric Berne's game, "Now I've Got You, You S.O.B." Try buying a house or a car and expect the salesman to admit he knows what you meant if you didn't spell it out very carefully and in writing.

Let's try a little exercise. Here are different versions of a rule you might introduce in your home. You decide which is most definable:

A. Sandy must mow the lawn before she goes to ball practice.
B. Sandy must mow the lawn and trim the edges at the sidewalk before she goes to ball practice.
C. Sandy must mow the lawn, trim the edges at the sidewalk, sweep the walk, and put the lawn mower back in its place before she goes to ball practice.

Assuming you expected the walk swept and the mower put away, I hope you chose letter "C" as the most definable. And believe it or not, it's the one children prefer, because they know exactly what they must do to earn the praise, "That's a good job." They *want* to please you. This way, they know they're not going to get a hassle from you, so they can relax. In addition, they'll feel that they're competent mowers of lawn, and this will boost their sense of safety, security, and stability and their sense of self-esteem as well.

Let's try another. Which is most definable?

A. Terry must clean his room before dinner.
B. Terry must clean his room before he gets to *eat* dinner.
C. Terry must make his bed neatly, line up his shoes under the foot of the bed, put all the laundry in the laundry basket, and adjust his blinds before he gets to eat dinner.

Try making these more definable:
* Merrilee may not wear her skirts too short.
* Neddy should get his bath early.
* Orson should do his homework after school.
* Penelope may not date until she's older.

You get the idea.

But The Fewer Rules The Better

"Wait," you protest. "This is too much trouble. I want our lives simplified, not filled with rules laid upon rules."

Right! You don't want many rules. Thomas Jefferson taught, "That government governs best which governs least." Parents should be Jeffersonians even if the politicians aren't.

The beauty of it is, you don't *need* many rules. Once you've got one good rule ironed out, children seem to behave better all around, and troubles that you had with them in other respects seem to fade away and not need rules.

Back to Ilene and Kenny. I asked her to what she attributed the turnaround in his behavior. "It was the rule," she said. Notice: "the" rule. She had imposed only one rule: "Kenny, when you get in your jammies you must put your dirty clothes in the laundry hamper."

That's it. That was all. No long list of "thou shalts and shalt nots." No constitution with articles and clauses and sub-clauses. Only one rule! But hang on. There was a little more to it, as we'll see in a bit.

Chore Rules and Freedom For Mom

As long as we're talking about defining rules and cleaning rooms, would you like to know how to emancipate yourself from ever cleaning his room again? It takes less than ten days, and then you're free for the next fifteen years.

You start alone or sitting at the kitchen table with the kid. You need a sheet of blank paper or light cardboard and a dark pencil or marker.

"Vickie, I want to figure out how to make your room really nice and clean. Would you like to help me do this?"

Vickie could be suspicious and decline, in which case you continue without her. Or, she is flattered that you want to include her and sits down.

"Let's pretend your room is really a mess, and we want to make it so clean you can brag about it to Grandma. What's the first thing we could do?

"Make the bed?" Vickie suggests.

"Good," you respond, writing on the paper, "'Make the bed without wrinkles.'" If the child can't read, write it anyway and draw a stick figure in the left margin of someone making a bed.

"What should be next?" you ask.

"Put the dirty clothes in the laundry basket?"

"Good idea," you answer, writing and sketching on the paper. What's next?"

"Line up the shoes under the bed," says Vickie.

"Line up shoes neatly at the foot of the bed," goes

on the paper.

"Pick up the stuff on the floor."

"Pick. . . up. . . loose. . . things. . . on. . . the. . . floor," you write.

"Straighten the closet," is her next suggestion.

"'Make things in the closet neat.' What's next?"

"I don't know."

"How about straightening and dusting the bureau top?"

"Oh, yeah. That."

"Closing the drawers and closet door?"

"Okay. That, too."

"Adjusting the blinds?"

"Uh huh."

"And emptying the trash basket."

"Yeah."

"Vickie, this looks great. Let's go up to your room. I'm going to do these things and you read them to me so that I'll be sure to get them all."

Now, all of the above comes under "definable" in the criteria for a good rule. Part two of this little exercise comes under the second characteristic, "reasonable."

2. REASONABLE

Four characteristics of a good rule—the first is that it must be "definable," and the second that it be "reasonable."

Is it reasonable to expect that a five-year old child can clean his own room as well as described above with Vickie? Not unless he's carefully taught. Here is how to teach him. Follow this technique and you will avoid the complaints and tantrums you'd have otherwise.

"Okay, Vickie. Here are a couple of thumbtacks. Hang your list on the inside of your closet door. Try to get it straight so it will look neat. . . .Good. Now, you read them to me and I'll do them."

"Make the bed without wrinkles," the child reads from the list or from the stick figures in the left margin.

You, mom, make the bed, and fuss with it a bit so that she sees how important this is. Old army dads will probably use hospital corners and finish with bouncing a quarter in the middle, but that's just showing off.

"Okay," you announce. "What's next?"

Vickie reads, "Put the dirty clothes in the laundry basket."

You, mom (or dad), do that and then ask, "What's next?"

"Line up the shoes under the bed," she answers.

You do that, mom. "What's next?"

"Pick up loose things on the floor."

Do it, mom.

"Straighten the closet."

Do this, too.

"Straighten and dust the bureau top."

Done.

"Close the drawers and closet door."

Yes.

"Adjust the blinds."

Okay.

"Empty the trash basket."

"You do that one, Vickie."

Tomorrow: "Come on, Vickie. Let's go clean your room. You read me the list."

This is great, she thinks! (Heh, heh, little does she know.)

This day, she reads the list and you do the chores—all except the last two, "Adjust the blinds," and "Empty the trash basket."

"You do that, Vickie."

The third day, you do all but the last three. The fourth day, she does the last four. Each day, she reads and does one more item from the bottom of the list. If you've got ten items on the list, she has either seen you do them or done them herself ten times. On the last day she does them all herself.

Can she now clean the room in the manner you've defined? Yes. The rule is definable and reasonable.

One of the most important reasons children have a hard time with chore rules is that they really don't know how to do them. Haven't you ever had a task so overwhelming you just couldn't get started?

Don't you remember putting off that term paper when you were in school? It wasn't because you wanted to spend the entire last day and night before it was due in a panicked attempt to pull something together. It wasn't because you hated the topic—your instructor may even have let you choose that. It was because you just didn't quite understand how it was to be done.

I remember struggling months and months on a master's thesis, never really quite confident of what I was doing. If my advisor had known that I didn't even understand the format, he could have cleared it up for me in five minutes, and my thesis would have been half the hassle it was. When I was finished I was amazed! That's it? That's all there is to it? I could do another in just a few weeks if I had to.

Since then I've changed clutches, replaced brakes, plumbed, wired, painted, roofed, and built a couple of whole houses, mostly with a dummies' guide in one hand and a tool in the other. If you know what is to be done (definable) and how you can do it (reasonable), you—and your child—can do almost anything.

Unfortunately, as parents and caregivers, we often overestimate our children's experience and underestimate their intelligence.

Your teachers didn't know that you didn't know how. It was clear to *them*. Everything is difficult at first, and everything is clear if you've done it once. Maybe twice. Or with Vickie, ten times or so.

Of course, some rules are not reasonable because of the child's maturity. I know a third grade teacher who allows no talking whatsoever after the opening bell and before lunch. That's about three hours. Three hours for an eight-year-old not to talk? The teacher gets her silence, but it's a joyless class, and I think the rule is unreasonable.

Are you really going to ground your child for six weeks because he got a "D"? One "D," six long weeks?

Are you going to forbid your daughter from dating a local boy until she's eighteen? Or, have you ever said, "You sit there until you've finished your dinner!" But ten-year-old taste buds perceive brussel sprouts quite differently than do thirty-year-old taste buds.

Be reasonable. If you're determined to ground the student, how about grounding until he has a note from his teacher that his grade average has improved? Or allow the daughter to date earlier under somewhat monitored conditions. Or requiring only that the child "try a taste" of everything served at dinner?

We used the latter rule. "You must try a bite of everything served." Oh, the drama, the entertainment value you can get from a single lima bean! Gasp, grimmace, groan, choke. Our rationale was that as children grow up, their tastes grow up, too, and they won't know when that happens if they don't keep trying. It seemed reasonable.

3. ENFORCEABLE

This is a little awkward. First of all, you might not really *want* to enforce the rule. If the child senses that it will be inconvenient for you to enforce it, this will be the signal for him to test your resolve. Or, it may be that he can break the rule and you won't know it. Either way, the rule is unenforceable.

Suppose your rule is that he must finish his chore or no dessert. This is the day you've made his favorite, Key Lime Pie. You worked hard on it, it turned out beautifully, and you're anxious to have him try it. He knows this, so this will be the day he neglects the chore. Do you really want to enforce the rule? No, but you'd better, and in a little bit we'll talk about how this is done.

But first, remember our thesis that we're using rules to provide safety, security, and stability for the child. If you won't know every time he breaks a rule, then his world becomes inconsistant, and he will have to break other rules until he finally finds one that *is* enforced.

Is the following rule enforceable?

"Winona, you're not allowed to wear lipstick until you're fifteen."

Well, will you know each and every time she breaks that rule? No way. As soon as she gets on the school bus her girlfriend will give her the lipstick she carries for her. The rule is broken and no safety, security, or stability value is gained. Worse, she'll feel bad about the rule, feel bad about herself for breaking it, and feel bad toward you because you're so ineffective as a parent.

What should you do? Simply, you can't make this a rule. But you can let her know how you feel. You might say, "Winona, I really don't want to see you wearing lipstick before you're fifteen, and I hope you won't wear it at school, either."

Now she knows what is expected of her. Your wishes are definable and you think they're reasonable, but because they're not enforceable you can't make them a rule. If she chooses to go against your wishes, she may be at odds with you but neither you nor your wishes have lost power.

Let's try another example. "Xavier, you're not allowed to hit your sister!"

Definable? Yes. Reasonable? Yes. Enforceable? No. The child will mutter to the girl, "Just wait 'til I get you outside."

So, do you let the boy persecute the little sister? Of course not. But what can you do? You can't make this a rule for it can be broken with impunity.

About the best you can do is, "Xavier, I don't want to ever see you hitting your sister. And I hope you won't be a sneak and a bully by doing it when I'm not around."

There may be other problems when you depend on others' testimonies that a rule has been broken. What happens when little sister Yvonne comes crying that her brother has been shoving her? Did he really? Probably, but you didn't see it, and you don't know what preceded it. And before you come crashing down around his head, consider—just consider— this scenerio.

It's been a long, rainy Saturday afternoon. The kids have been cooped up at home for hours and are bored out of their skulls. "Why don't you read a good book?" you suggest. "There's that nice book Aunt Zelda got you for your birthday that you never read."

Sitting in the family room, Yvonne taunts her brother. "What are you going to get Amy for her birthday?"

"Why should I get her anything?"

"Well, you like her so much, don't you?"

"No! I don't like her! She looks like a squirrel."

"Yes you do! I see the way you look at her every

time you pass her in the hall."

"What do you mean? I don't look at her *any* way in the hall."

"I see it all the time. You're really zapped by her. I'm going to put a note in her locker telling her that you want to know what she wants for her birthday."

"You better not! I'll whack you one up alongside the head!"

"No you won't. See, I'm writing it now. 'Dear Amylove: What. . .can. . .I. . .get. . .you. . .for. . .'"

"Hey, stop that! Gimme that. Come on. . ."

"No! Get away! Mom, Xav is shoving me!"

And you, innocent parent, have been sucked in once again to bring life to an otherwise boring day.

There's more. A child who can get others into trouble by reporting them is in a tough situation. He's in the middle. You say, "You should have told me." On the other side, the child may be suffering localized terrorism: "You tell and I'll get you!"

What do you do when a child reports on another? It's best to ignore the report in front of the child. "I'm sorry, dear, but I wasn't there," and refuse to be appointed judge over who struck who first. But you can file it away and keep an eye out for what's going on in the future.

When children have the responsibility to report on each other they may learn amateur extortion: "You do it my way or I'll tell Mom you've been hitting me." Now you're fostering some really unpleasant characteristics.

What's a poor parent or teacher to do? Just don't make rules which depend on the testimony of others to insure their enforcement. You can make your wishes known, you can use persuasion and express your hopes. But don't make rules which can be broken without your personally knowing.

Here's a classic. "You can't watch television until you've finished your homework." Definable and reasonable, yes. But enforceable?

"I don't have any homework. I did it in study hall. I finished it on the bus." Do you really know if this is true? The rule is unenforceable.

Instead, how about, "You must have ninety minutes of study time before bedtime. When would you like to have it?"

"But I don't have any homework tonight."

"That's nice. Now you can get a head start on the exams. When would you like to have your ninety minutes study time?"

"I left all my books at school."

"Oh, good. I've been wanting to give you one of my favorite books to read for your study time. It's about the coming of the Civil War, which is the kind of thing you're learning at school."

"Uh, wait a minute. I can probably borrow Brady's times tables from next door. I need to get the nines and the twelves better. And I think I can get started on my health project."

"Whatever," you reply lightly.

The bottom line: A good rule must definable, reasonable, and enforceable. By enforceable, we mean that you should be willing to enforce it, and that you will know every time the rule is broken without having to depend on someone else to tell you.

4. Consequence for Disobeying

Many parents and teachers have rules, but they don't have consequences. "Class, please be quiet," Ms. Carson asks.

"Class, I asked you to be quiet."

"Class, settle down and be quiet!"

"I'm not going to tell you again, please be quiet!"

"How many times do I have to tell you to be quiet!!"

"I'm not going to ask you again, 'How many times do you have to be told to be quiet?'!"

"BeeEEEEE QUI-yet!!!"

And with vein standing out on her forehead, hands trembling in exasperation, broken pencil in hand, she gets her quiet.

But it only lasts until the class realizes they're not going to get to see Ms. Carson have a stroke, nor is anything going to happen to them. Then it's back to whispers, mumbling, and a general undertone of talking punctuated by an occasional wimpish plea from the teacher, "I'm not going any further until you can stop talking."

Smith and Smith, on whose fine work in consistency training this technique is based, did not include a consequence as a necessary element of a good rule. You were supposed to just simply enforce it. And their procedure worked—in a way, in a sort of a way.

However, our experience over the years was that this led to awful knock-down and drag out hassles that exhausted everyone, children included. In fact, I came to believe that the hassles may even have been rewarding to the child. "You ruined my evening by insisting on a bedtime, so now I'll ruin yours, ha, ha, ha."

Rule Testing

We're suggesting that good rules can bring a child safety, security, and stability. But this won't happen unless the child knows the rule will be enforced. How can he find out if your rule will be enforced? He must test it. That is, he must break it to see if the expected consequence will occur.

This means that you can expect the child to break the rule. Don't be angry. He's just testing. And he will be disappointed—perhaps unconsciously—if you don't apply the consequence. We'll talk about how strongly he'll test the rule in the next chapter. Brace yourself.

But all of this means that whatever consequence you choose must be one you are willing to live with. If your rule is that Dominic must finish his study time or he won't be permitted to attend Scouts on Tuesday evenings, know that the day will come when he'll test that rule.

But you want him to go to Scouts. It's a great program, and if he makes Eagle he'll have a major accomplishment which will give him satisfaction all his life. Dom knows you want him to attend and he will test the rule. Will you enforce it?

You'd better, because if you let it slide he'll lose safety, security, and stability, and he'll have to test another rule to see if that will be enforced. If the second rule fails, he'll go on and on, testing (breaking) rules until in exasperated desperation you finally draw the line.

Building a consequence into your rules frees everyone from hassles. You should make them automatic. You avoid warnings, and perhaps even reminders. Let the rule be the ogre, not you.

Suppose your rule is that Ellie must hang up her coat when she comes in, or she must remain in for the rest of the evening.

"Ah, Ellie, you left your coat on the couch again. Too bad. That means you're in for the evening. You won't be able to go to K-Mart with me after supper. What was that shampoo you wanted? Maybe I can find it for you by myself."

Definable? Yes. Reasonable? Yes. Enforceable? Yes. Consequence? Yes. It's a good rule, and may be the only one you'll need to see a sudden improvement in other behavior as well.

Try another. "Francie must finish her dinner or she gets no dessert."

Is that *definable*? Yes, if you mean she must clean her plate. No, if you really mean that she needs to eat just a litle bit of each thing, or if you'll settle for having had the food stirred around somewhat.

Is this rule *reasonable*? Yes, if Francie took her own portions. No, if you heaped piles of your favorite Chef Prudhomme's speecy-spicy Cajun rice on her plate.

Is it *enforceable*? Yes, if you're there to see her eat it. No, if she can feed it to the family dog while you're in the kitchen, or if the baby-sitter has to decide.

Is there a *consequence*? Yes, no dessert.

So, we've got a good rule. Now, will the child accept the consequence without a hassle? No, she'll test your resolve, and there's a very effective technique for handling her rule-testing. We'll get to that in the next chapter.

But first, what about incidental things you'd like the child to do for which you have no rule? This is where you insert *"command rules."*

A Word about Command Rules

Even though you're working toward getting the child independent, there will be times when you'll want him to do something on the spur of the moment. These are "command rules," and there are two important caveats to watch for.

The first is courtesy. If courtesy is the oil that lubricates civilization, it's even better than Teflon for families. Haven't you found that most people will give way when we ask for something kindly? This is a valuable social skill children can learn from us.

"Greg, there's another bag of groceries in the car. Will you bring them in for me, please?" Contrast that with "Get the rest of the groceries, and don't drop anything." The first is still a "command rule," even if you phrase it so that it doesn't sound like a command.

Here's another. "Harry, the Iversons are coming over Saturday afternoon. Do you suppose you could have the lawn done before they arrive?" Or is "I want that lawn done by noon on Saturday!" just as good? You know it's not, because you don't respond well to the latter type yourself.

This is all good manners, I'm sure, but it's also good psychology. Low threat commands, even though they may have quiet, hidden power behind them, seem to be internalized more effectively than high threat commands. We're not entirely sure why this works, but I think it has something to do with Leon Festinger's Theory of Cognitive Dissonance. When we apply it to children, it goes something like this.

If a child is required to do something he doesn't want to do, and there's a harsh punishment if he doesn't, he will find every way he can to thwart the punishment before he finally gives in and does what's required. And when it's over, he still won't want to do it next time.

On the other hand, if he is required to do something he doesn't want to do, and there's the threat of mild punishment, when he finally does it he wonders, "Why am I doing this?" His actions (doing it) and his desires (not doing it) are out of harmony—dissonant—and this is unpleasant. To resolve the dissonance in his mind, he decides he's doing it because he *wants* to do it.

This may be why volunteers for the Peace Corps or ambulance squads or small town fire companies are so dedicated. "Why am I doing this? I guess because I really believe in it and want to."

I submit that when your child does his duty because he wants to do it, he's independent and you have done your parenting job well.

The trick, of course, is to make the unpleasantness of the consequence just a shade stronger than is the pleasure of breaking the rule. You may have to do some fine tuning here by adjusting the level of punishment.

It's also best to keep the consequence quietly in the background. You don't fine tune the rule by constantly reminding the child about the reality of the punishment. You don't want him to obey because you nag him. You want him to obey because he has chosen to do so.

For example, here are five different levels of threat. Which is the highest?

"Jack, you know you're not allowed to talk while the teacher is talking."

"Jack, if you continue talking, you're going to get a detention."

"Jack, do you want to sit here in this room after school while all your friends are going home or trying out for the team?"

"Jack, you'd better have someone call your parents, because you're going to be in detention so long tonight you'll to be late to dinner!"

"Listen, Jocko, I've about had it with you. I'm going to fix your wagon good if you don't shut your mouth and keep it shut!"

Yes, the last is what we call "high threat," and as you've probably found, it doesn't work very well. Consider the same scene in "low threat."

"Kelly, please don't talk while I'm talking."

Now, Kelly is a bubbly child and forgets easily. When she makes just a short, quiet whisper a second time, the teacher catches her eye, smiles slightly and says, "Kelly, please don't talk." (I know, that *is* a reminder, isn't it?)

Kelly catches herself, sits up straight, and tries mightily to obey. However, after a few minutes something strikes her fancy and she's at it again.

"Kelly, see me after school, please. Now when the Rough Riders saw the gunners firing down from their positions on San Juan Hill, Teddy Roosevelt brought his horse up to the front lines and. . ."

That's all. No muss, no fuss. No irritation, no harrangs. Just quietly and politely, "See me after school, please." The consequence has been applied. If Kelly raises a stink about this, you may find yourself in a "power play," and we'll fix that also in the next chapter. But my experience has been that a quiet, courteous application of the consequence is all in takes in most cases.

The second important caveat with command rules is that you draw the line in the sand very clearly. If the child steps over it just a little, you'll know and so will he, real fast. That is, if you have asked that something be done, you want it done exactly, quickly and without a hassle. If you're generous, as was Kelly's teacher, you might remind the child once, because she *is* just a child and forgets easily. But never tell the child three times.

Laurie has three children and a van. Sometimes the kids get so boisterous while they're riding along she can hardly think. So she calls out for all to hear, "It's too loud in here."

The noise lessens considerably, but in a minute or so it's back up to the original level. Here comes the reminder: "It's too loud in here."

Ah, quiet. But not for long. Mike is trying to establish his natural male dominance over Nicole, and Nicole is having none of it. "Owww, you punched me! Mom, Nicole punched me!"

Here comes the command rule. No need to shout— just loud enough to be heard. "All right, that's it. Don't touch each other, and no more talking until I say so."

Notice the beauty of this. No more talking means no more arguing, no more testimony about who did what to whom, no more calls for judgement.

Remember also, the line has been drawn very clearly. No more talking means no talking. None. Nothing. Zilch. Zip. Zed. Once the children understand you mean exactly that, that's what you'll get.

But the first time you try this, they'll push it. After a couple of minutes, Mike will venture, "Move your foot."

Careful, Mom. This is a test. Will you allow Mike's mild comment? After all, it is a lot quieter, and they *have* been obedient for a little while. You're

67

tempted to let it pass, because if Nicole is fooling around with her feet, Mike should be able to point that out. You did tell her, didn't you, that they weren't to touch each other?

No, this is rule testing. Mike is less interested in Nicole's foot than in what you will do. This is the first tentative effort to see if you really mean what you said.

You call back, "I said no talking until I say it's okay." That's the reminder, because they're kids and you're not an ogre.

Silence. For another couple of minutes. Then, from the back seat, a whispered "Gimme that!"

Okay, Mom, never tell them three times. We're into consequence. You have got to move. You have got to apply a consequence, and you've got to apply it now.

What is your consequence? Since this is a command rule, you really don't have one worked out and published, so you'll have to pull one out of the hat. It doesn't matter a whole lot what it is, just so that it's slightly more unpleasant than are the joys of hassling sisters in the car.

You could call back, "Mike, when we get home you go to your room until I say you can come out." Or, "Mike, there'll be no television for you tonight." Or, whatever.

In our house, or rather in our car, when the children were younger, I would simply pull the car off the road on to the shoulder. I'd check the traffic carefully and get out. I'd walk around to the curb side, open the door, and gently but firmly pull the offender out. Then I'd apply one quick whack on the behind, put the child back, close the door, walk carefully around to the drivers side, and pull the car back into traffic. No shouting, no recriminations, no humiliations. After a few minutes of silence from the kids, I'd call back, "I guess you can talk quietly now if you want."

Today, I hear those same children, now grown, call out to my grandchildren, "It's too loud in here." And we grin at each other over the sudden calm.

To Spank or Not to Spank

I guess the time has come to talk about spanking as a consequence. You may not agree with spanking. Well, you're in good company. One of the finest mothers I know of—Emma Riggs McKay—never spanked her children. In fact, B.F. Skinner used to say that if you're really good at child management you never have to use punishment at all. I've never been that good. We'll talk more about Skinner and his techniques in Part Two of this book.

I do know of parents who don't spank, but who do use heavy guilt trips to manipulate their children. "All right, Ozzie, if you can't do what I say I'm going to turn around right now and we're going right back home, and no one will get to play in the park and it will be all your fault. Is that what you want? Do you want to be the one who will ruin it for everybody?" And the parent feels virtuous because she doesn't spank. That's awful.

I've known parents who will send their kids to Coventry. That's a term from England, where the townspeople of Coventry hated soldiers and wouldn't speak to them or acknowledge their presence. Being sent to Coventry was a punishment for slothful soldiers. In child rearing, it's refusing to speak to the child as a consequence for disobedience. A young woman told me once that it was not unusual for her parents to stop talking to her for two or three days at a time. This is preferred over spanking?

Or just being angry is used as a consequence. There are parents who will stalk around in a huff, hurling occasional insults at the child and muttering about his inadequacies for hours. I think that's much worse than spanking if the spanking is done right.

The reason I used spanking occasionally is because it can be immediate, short, and over with in a hurry. If it's used judiciously, the child will even prefer it over some other methods.

If you had been the child Mike in the back seat, which would you have preferred—a quick swat on the behind, or being banished from the TV all evening? A moment of disapproval and embarrassment, or carrying the expectation of an impending punishment all afternoon?

I find that one swat usually clears the air, and if I do it right at the moment the child steps over my line in the sand instead of waiting until I get angry, everybody— including the child—is happier. He's paid his debt to society, you speak to him kindly afterward (not an apology), and life moves ahead.

Now, I'm not talking about child abuse. Child abusers, depending on the situation, either need special help or a special hell, and at another time I might go on at great length about child abuse. I'm talking here about a quick, effective, humane method of helping children learn obedience.

For the most part, I think an occasional quick spat on the behind is all that's necessary. Tell them once, remind them quietly if needed, and then apply the consequence. Never tell them a third time!

If the consequence is a spank, once on the padded wide expanse of pain sensors on the buttocks should do the trick. If the disobedience has been really bad, perhaps two spanks with your open palm. If it's been outrageous and you really want to impress the child, three. But any more than that and you're slipping into abuse. Your adrenalin will start pumping and you'll be more severe than you intended.

After all, you are much larger and stronger than the child, and what may have begun as an attention getting consequence can degenerate into a beating. Not good. Bad. The first three spanks may benefit the child; the fourth just satisfies—or even stimulates—your anger.

Remember, if you do apply the consequence close to your "line in the sand," you'll more likely be calm and rational if you do resort to spanking.

Do we have to say anything about spanking with an object? "Peter, bring me the strap!" Oh, no, please. The open palm of your hand gives some feedback to you on the spanking. Straps, hairbrushes, rulers—none of these will make the spanking more effective, and I believe they are cruel.

What if you give the child a spat on the behind and he blurts out, "Din't hurt!" You respond quietly, "Oh, that's too bad. It was supposed to hurt. I guess I'll have to try again." Whack.

After the third time he says this, you've used up your spanking limit and you'll have to try something else, like loss of privileges, grounding, or time out in his room. More on "time out" in Part Two of this book.

There will be social workers from your local child welfare department who will disagree strongly with my views on spanking. They would have you sit down with your child and reason with him as if he were an adult about concepts his little Piagetian brain isn't mature enough to handle.

You have probably read and tried techniques which sound beautifully idealistic, written over the past thirty years by psychologists who are filled with compassion for the children. Do their hopes match their experience? Is it your understanding these programs have worked? Or have you felt the children never learned that their behavior has consequences, that they're responsible for their behavior, and that their behavior needs to be improved or their lives will be impaired?

When the experts who have dominated the field for the past generation can demonstrate more effective techniques than those I propose, I'll revise my position on spanking.

Getting Children to Sleep

We've talked about routines to give children a sense of safety, security, and stability. Bedtime routines are excellent for this purpose, so long as they don't become a major production which dominates the life of the parents.

I believe that one of the reasons children need more sleep than adults is that adults need some waking time away from the children. Having been with them for fourteen hours straight, you do need a couple of more hours to yourself or in the company of another adult.

We generally have techniques for getting to sleep ourselves. My mother always had a book by her bedside, and she would read until her eyes got heavy. Others can't let go until they see Jay Leno's monologue through their toes. Others. . .well, most everybody has something that works for them.

But babies sometimes have difficulty in going to sleep because they don't have a technique. They don't know *how* to go to sleep, and they lie there in the crib and cry and cry until you come in and pick them up and walk them around and pat them on the back and coo at them. Then they fall asleep, and you lower them gently into the crib and hope to escape before they realize they're not being carried around nestled against your shoulder.

Do you see what's happening? You have taught them that the way to go to sleep is by being carried. But what you really want is for them to go to sleep alone in their crib.

Perhaps you should put them down in the crib and then sit beside them and comfort them until they finally go to sleep. This will work, but it will require your sitting beside them every night comforting them, and if they're not particularly tired, you may fall asleep before they do.

What to do? Here is a technique that will teach them to go to sleep in their cribs in three days, perhaps four. But you'll have to follow it carefully or you'll blow the whole thing and it will take three weeks, or maybe never.

Decide when you want Baby to go to sleep. Eight o'clock? Whatever. A little while before bedtime, pick him up pleasantly and let him know he's in for a nice, quiet time with you. Minimal stimulation, maximum soothing. Clean him up. Change his diapers. Into pajamas. Nursing or body contact while on the bottle. Softly, gently, into bed. Covers up. Quiet kiss. Tiptoe out and close the door.

If this is Day One, Baby will cry in disbelief. How dare! Banished from the real world, while others are still up and the television is still going strong. His egocentric outrage will be beyond anything you thought possible. Sit still, Mom. Cover your ears, Dad.

After a while you won't be able to stand it. Maybe he's got his head stuck between the slats in the crib. Maybe there's a diaper pin sticking him. You've got to check.

Of course you must. But do it simply, matter-of-factly, with no muss and no fuss. Don't turn the light on. Stumble in quietly and check him. Pick him up and gently put him down. Cover up. No hug, no kiss. No criticism, no comfort. Slip out the door and close it.

Baby will cry for another ten minutes before your nuturing hormones demand that you see that he's okay. Slip in again. Without a word, put him down and pull the cover up. Out quietly, door closed.

In another ten minutes, Baby will be exhausted. He will whimper a while, and your hopes will rise. Soon, all will be quiet, and you'll want to check again just to enjoy the sight of him finally asleep.

Figure forty minutes for the first night, assuming you're strong enough to resist picking him up and comforting him. If you're not, this could continue until ten o'clock, and he won't learn that it's possible to go to sleep by himself in his own crib.

If you're in an apartment with paper-thin walls, or if you're sharing a home with his grandmother, you may have to advise these neighbors that you're beginning "consistency training through bedtime routine," and you expect it will take three nights to accomplish it. This sounds professional and will keep them in their place until you've done it.

The second night, plan on twenty minutes of protest from Baby.

The third night, he'll be down to five minutes.

The fourth night, there'll be only a few whimpers.

The fifth night, he'll go down with a smile.

Older children—ages one through twelve—may require a little more ingenuity, but the principles remain the same.

"Whew! They're down," we sigh as we sink into the recliner at eight o'clock.

But are they down? In many homes there's another two hours of calling up and down the stairs, pitter-pattering in the upstairs hall, and heart-rending whimpers about monsters under the bed. We need a bedtime rule that's definable, reasonable, enforceable, and has a consequence.

How's this for a good rule? "You must have washed your face and hands, brushed your teeth, gotten in your jammies, had your prayers, and said your last word by eight o'clock, or tomorrow night you must be in bed a half hour earlier."

That's got all the elements of a good rule, but perhaps the "reasonable" element needs special attention. How old are the children? Is eight o'clock a reasonable bedtime for ten or eleven year old? Should children be required to be in bed before the sun goes down and while their friends are still playing outside? Should a ten year old be expected to go to bed at the same time as a five year old?

Perhaps children could get a half hour tacked on to their bedtimes at each birthday after age six. Perhaps summertime or weekend bedtimes could be different from school night bedtimes.

Further, it may be unreasonable to expect a child to leave the kick-soccer game at ten 'til eight, race up the stairs, run through his routine, and then go to sleep while his heart is still pounding and the adrenalin in his bloodstream hasn't metabolized yet.

Many families have found a half hour "reading time" effective. Bedtime may be at eight, but if the child wants he may keep his light on and read until eight thirty. This is not play time, not talk time, not wander-around-the-bedroom time. This is reading time.

"I don't want to read now."

"That's all right, you don't have to. Good night. Lights out."

"Wait! Let me get my book!"

"Okay."

In half an hour, the excitement of the game will have died away, the pulse slowed, and chances are the child will have drifted off to sleep with his book on his chest.

This has some serendipitous effects. The child gets practice at reading and will become one of the Bluebirds in his school reading groups. And do you know how many books you can read in just thirty minutes a night? By the time you're no longer monitoring bedtimes he'll have read the junior classics and all of the fun books you read as a child. Never mind that you're down in the living room watching yet another rerun of "Cheers."

We mentioned the child's "last word" as part of a bedtime routine. This is a device designed to keep you from being bugged to death by the child's ingeneous observations through the rest of your evening.

In our house, it went like this. Hands and face washed, jammies on, prayers with Mom or Dad by the bed, and then, "What's your last word?" That is, what is the last thing you're going to say before tomorrow morning? Say it now or forever hold your peace.

It was usually something like, "Are we going to the shore this summer?" Answer: "We've been thinking about it. Good night." Or, "I've got to have a dozen cup cakes for school tomorrow." Argh! But that was it. Nothing more. One word, one spank.

Sometimes a child would appear on the stairway and point with great animation upstairs. Now it's time for Charades. He's got something he's just bursting to tell, but he doesn't want the spank.

"Is the baby okay?"

He nods vigorously, points again upstairs.

"Is the toilet still running?"

The head shakes. Hand signals.

"Hopping. Richard's hopping on the bed."

No, the head indicates. Finally he can stand it no more and blurts out, "There's a cricket under my bed!"

Ah. So it's upstairs with the broom, find the cricket, sweep him out, crunch. Yuck. Flush.

But what's the rule? One word, one spank. It's time. Come here for your spank.

And while the child's eyes are squeezed shut and his arms are rigid at his sides, you lean over and give him the lightest of pats on the rear end. He breathes a sigh of relief and grins, but doesn't talk. You give him a hug and tuck him in again, and go back downstairs.

Was the rule followed? Yes. Will he take advantage of you like this again? No, because he knows the spank was light with a mercy that may not be repeated. But he's got the safety, security, and stability out of the deal, and you've had a warm little adventure together.

The Family Bed

I recall a mother who inadvertantly had taught her child that he could go to sleep only when she laid down in his bed with him. Other parents have had their children climb into bed with them—not just after bad dreams or during thunderstorms, but every night, for years.

I have my own feelings about this. Both my wife and I have a strong need for privacy, and our bedroom is our private place. By simple unannounced practice we have always locked our bedroom door. If a child knocks, we get up and let him in.

But this is unique. Through most of history and in much of the world, families sleep in a family bed, all curled up like puppies and sprawled out across each other. Some argue that this brings comfort and security to children which lasts all their lives.

I'm impressed by the persuasion of a mother from Minnesota, Tine Thevenin, who twenty years ago wrote "The Family Bed," in which she cited case after case of parents who have opened their beds to their children. Ashley Montagu, Margaret Mead, and Jane Goodall, among others, endorsed Thevenin's crusade.

More impressive to me is the enthusiasm of parents who have tried it, as compared to mere theorists. After all, the real experts in child psychology are the professional mothers—thoughtful, intelligent practioners of the craft—and their responsible partners, the fathers.

Her thesis contradicts my techniques for getting babies and children to sleep. But perhaps she is right. Perhaps children benefit from the warm body contact of others all night. Maybe a family bed produces more stable and confident children.

If you can't accept my counsel for helping babies and children get to sleep, track down Thevenin's book and consider it carefully. It's the other end of the spectrum.

This much I do know. The techniques I've described for settling children down in three days do work, and they give parents a respite from the burdens of parenting.

I also know that the middle of the spectrum—that is, parents' walking the baby endlessly or constantly attending to cries in the nursery—is frustrating to both parents and children. It's the worst of three possible worlds.

Chapter 6— What To Expect:
The Sequence Of Success

We have suggested that a few good rules—the fewer the better—can bring your children safety, security, and stability, which in turn will satisfy very important basic needs and free them to take the necessary risks for success in their lives ahead of them.

We described in detail the characteristics of a good rule, that it be definable, reasonable, enforceable, and that it have a consequence.

Now, what can you expect when you introduce your new rule? This is amazing. I can predict with about 85% confidence, that this is what you'll get from the children.

1. Initial compliance
2. Horrendous initial rule-testing
3. Short-term compliance
4. Milder secondary rule-testing
5. Long-term compliance
6. Rule-testing whenever the environment changes.

Here it is graphed to make it stand out:

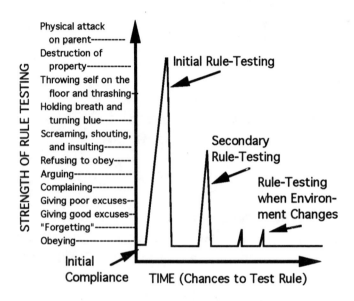

Initial Compliance

Let's start at the beginning. "Quentin, we've got a new rule. From now on, you need to feed the dog before you have supper."

"Yeah, okay."

That's it? No arguments, no hassle, no complaints? Remember, children really want rules, and you can expect that they'll accept them initially. This is wonderful! You should have done this long ago. But stand back, because in the next step you won't believe the hassle you're going to get.

Horrendous Initial Rule-Testing

In spite of the child's surprising acceptance of the rule, he's going to have to test it to be sure he can depend on it. You do the same when you buy a new rope to help you take down an overgrown tree. You want to be sure it won't break when you cut heavy branches and lower them with the rope. You need confidence in the rope. You need safety, security, and stability. So you tie the rope way up there and pull. Then you hang on it, then swing on it. Yes, it's strong, and you can relax and feel confident.

Children, likewise, have to test a rule by trying to break it before they can be confident with it. Really, they hope they can't break it, just as you hope the rope will hold, even though they try as hard as they can.

There are two things you must do in handling initial rule-testing.

1. *Ask the child to restate the rule.*

Note, you try to avoid restating it yourself if you possibly can. This is important. It has something to do with cognitive dissonance, but we don't have to go into that here. Just try to get him to restate the rule.

2. *Ignore everything else.*

Don't respond to arguments. You can't win. The child lies awake at night constructing legal briefs worthy of a Philadelphia lawyer. You'll end up questioning your own wisdom and back off, while the child walks away grinning that once again he's wrapped you around his little finger.

Don't threaten with the consequence. You'll just inflame the situation into a terrible power play which will leave you exhausted, the child alienated, and the rest of the family in tears.

Don't stalk out of the room. That's retreat, and the child wins.

Don't sigh heavily and complain, "Oh, God, how long must I suffer with this child!" This equalizes the situation. You've ruined his evening and he's ruined yours. It's his payoff.

Do ask for a restatement of the rule, calmly and matter-of-factly. Ignore everything else. Don't get irritated. Scratch the dog's belly. Make a peanut butter cracker for yourself.

Back to Quentin's new rule. It's supper time and the family is coming in to eat. You wonder about the new rule and check on the dog. He hasn't been fed. Quentin is at the table.

"Uh, Quentin, what's the rule?"

"What rule?"

"The rule about the dog."

"Oh, that rule."

"Well, what's the rule?" Mildly, no irritation.

"I'll feed him after supper."

"What's the rule?"

"I told you, I'll feed him when I'm done."

"What's the rule?" Still mild, dispassionate.

"This is a stupid rule. The corn's going to get cold and Robert will get all the hot dogs in the beanie weenies."

You'll be tempted to get sucked into this and assure him that Mom will keep the corn in the pot and you'll see that Robert doesn't hoard all the hot dogs. Robert will then answer that he'd never do such a thing and that Quentin just hates him because he, Robert, gets better grades in math. Mom will say "Now, boys," and Sherry will say "Can't we just eat?" Quentin will have succeeded in shifting the focus from his shortcomings, or at least have irritated you in return for your having shamed him. Don't let this happen. Remember the first technique for handling rule-testing?

You simply reply, "What's the rule?"

Quentin answers, "Why am I the one who has to feed the dog? Everybody else plays with him. I don't even see him until he comes around here begging at the table. Sherry should be the one to feed him. She never does anything around here anyway."

Sherry cuts in, "I do so! I keep my room a lot cleaner than that pig pen you live in!"

Last week you might have gotten sidetracked and supported Sherry's analysis of Quentin's room, or chided her for insulting her brother, and the whole thing would have blown up in your face.

This week, having embarked on Making Rules That Stick, you ignore Sherry and respond, "What's the rule?"

Quentin will probably throw his napkin on the table,

stalk out to the cupboards, rattle and bang the dog's dish, and eventually come back to fling himself into his chair.

Last week you might have said, "Now, isn't that better? Now you can eat in peace and not have your chore hanging over your head," whereupon Quentin would have launched a tirade about how the family shouldn't have a dog in the first place and they spread germs and so on.

This week you're ignoring irrelevant behavior, which is everything but obeying the rule, so you continue your dinner table conversation without a break. "So, when is Grandma coming over?"

Of course, Quentin might have chosen to be really outrageous and continued the power struggle. You might have thrown up your hands and wondered why he would make such a protest out of a simple chore. You might have given up on Making Rules That Stick then and there. After all, your kids are different. What does some ivory-tower professor know about them? Truth be known, you can't wait until they're grown and gone and you can have some peace.

Don't you give up. This will work. Ask for a restatement of the rule and ignore irrelevant behavior. Of course, if the child breaks another rule by calling you a damned old bastard, you don't ignore that. You inflict the consequence, whatever it is, for cursing and talking mean to parents, real fast.

Let me offer a horror story—the worst I've ever heard—to illustrate how bad initial rule-testing can be. You may remember Tugboat Annie from an earlier chapter. She was the mother who had a thirteen year old daughter who was profane, smoked, drank, was promiscuous, and sometimes would stay out all night.

I was running a short course on "Improving Your Child's Behavior," and we had just finished discussing Definable, Reasonable, and Enforceable, qualities of a good rule. In those days I was leaning heavily on Smith and Smith's theories and had not yet discovered Consequence as the fourth element of a good rule. The class assignment was to develop a "good rule," and the following week we would review them and analyze them.

But at the next meeting, Annie (or whatever her name really was) came in shaking her head, "Wait 'til you hear what happened to me." She had gone ahead and instituted the rule. Of course, whatever I had planned was eclipsed, and nothing would do but for us to hear her experience.

Her rule was that Tricia must clean her room before she had dinner. Definable? Well, sort of. Reasonable? For a thirteen year old girl, yes. Enforceable? Yes, Mother would be there. Consequence? I wasn't teaching that back then.

Much to the mother's surprise, Tricia had accepted the new rule. "Yeah, okay." Initial compliance.

At dinner time, Annie asked her daughter, "How's your room?" I would have preferred that she checked first. Remember, you should know each and every time the rule has been broken without depending on someone else's testimony.

MAKING RULES THAT STICK

Tricia replied that it was "fine," but Annie didn't think so. She went upstairs to check and found it was a disaster area.

Back to the dinner table. "What's the rule?"

"Yeah, well, I'll clean it after dinner."

"What's the rule?"

"This is a stupid rule. Why all of a sudden new rules?"

"What's the rule?"

Tricia advised her mother where she could put her rules and that she didn't have to obey them and the mother couldn't make her.

Recall that there was no real consequence stated to the rule. The parent was simply to make sure it was obeyed. So Annie took the daughter by the wrist and headed for the bedroom. Tricia was kicking and screaming and banging on her mother's forearm, but up the stairs they went, bumpity-bump.

Annie thrust the girl into the bedroom and pulled the door closed. Tricia yanked it open. Annie pulled it closed. Yank, pull, yank, pull. Screams, profanity, threats from Tricia. Finally, silence. Yank. Pull.

Annie called down the stairs to the younger children, "Bring me a chair." And there she sat, clinging to the doorknob.

After a while, Tricia worked herself into another frenzy. Annie could hear items being swept off the bureau. Tricia would throw herself on the bed and scream and cry. Silence. Yank, pull.

Then it became apparent Tricia was pulling drawers out of the bureau and throwing them across the room.

Screams, sobs, and silence.

About ten o'clock, in the middle of a renewed tantrum, the daughter took a wooden chair and heaved it through the window, breaking glass and mullions together, with the chair landing on the lawn.

Ding-dong. "Mom, Mr. Urban wants to know if we're all right."

"We're all right, tell him we're all right."

Finally, Tricia fell asleep in the middle of the debris, and Mother spent the night asleep in the chair, clinging to the doorknob.

About six o'clock in the morning, Annie woke with Tricia opening the door. "I have to go to the bathroom!"

Annie answered (are you ready for this?), "What's the rule?" and pulled the door shut.

I guess there's something about not wetting your pants that's highly motivating to teenage girls. In any case, after a stunned silence, there was a scurrying around inside the room—sounds of the bed being put back upright, drawers being slid into place, and general rushing around.

Finally, "Room's clean!"

Annie peered in. It was, well, clean, in a way, in a sort of a way. "Okay."

Whoosh, across the hall and into the bathroom! Ahhhhhh.

By this time I was stunned. I had never expected anything like this. This was a class for ordinary parents with everyday kids, not for juvenile delinquents with severe behavioral disorders. This was terrible. I'd created a Frankinsteinian situation. Can professors be sued for malpractice?

"Annie, I am so sorry. I never meant for you to have to go through anything like that," I offered.

"Oh, no, it's just fine. Everything's fine."

"Fine?"

"Yes, she's fine now. Does what I ask, helps with the dishes. We talk. We've never talked before. She won't even smoke in the house because she knows I don't like it."

And for the rest of the short course, everything stayed fine.

I don't expect you're going to experience anything as traumatic as we saw at Tugboat Annie's house, but you can expect some rule-testing far beyond anything you thought reasonable. Brace yourself, and enlist the cooperation or understanding of others around you before it happens.

I have a theory here, and I don't want to say it the wrong way. But haven't you heard that when a cowboy wants to bring a young horse to saddle work, the horse jumps and bucks and does everything to get the cowboy off his back? When the rider is thrown, he's supposed to grab hold and get right back on again. It may take a while, but eventually the horse calms down and accepts the authority of the cowboy.

There's a term for this, but I don't want to use it in connection with children. I can just see some reviewer writing that Downing says you need to break your children to get them to behave.

Break their will, break their spirit, break their independence? Never! But if you mean that I believe children need to accept that there is someone in authority over them whom they must obey, yes, that's true.

This concept has been unpopular ever since the do-your-own-thing days of the Sixties. We have a "Free To Be Me" daycare center in our neighborhood. But the truth of life is that everybody's got a boss. Your foreman works under the manager, the manager works under the division head, the division head reports to the president, the president must please the board of directors, the board of directors are elected by the stockholders. The child must learn to work under authority or he'll have trouble all his life.

Lots of people say they don't want to have a boss. They're going to start their own business. But then the customers become their boss, and they end up working eighteen hours a day to meet their demands. Even farmers have to work under the requirements of natural laws such as the weather, crop rotation, or fertilizing techniques.

The world is a world of laws, and the sooner children accept this the easier it will be for them to use the laws to their own advantage and growth. Parents have an obligation to teach them this, and it can start with having to feed the dog before dinner.

Do you think Tricia was really happy, breaking the rules of society? I think she was out of control and knew it. I think she frightened even herself, knowing she would end up pregnant, diseased, and/or dead in a gutter somewhere, but she couldn't force herself to stop.

She got worse and worse, trying to find something she might do that was so outrageous her mother would sit up and say, "That's it! No more!" and take control of her.

I'm going to get in trouble for this, but as long as we're here, let me make this observation. I've known wives who wanted a take-charge type husband. Somehow they thought this was very masculine and it would make them feel more feminine. The husbands, however, would *not* take charge. It was, "Yes, dear, if that's what you really want." So they belittled and berated and humiliated their husbands, getting worse and worse, vainly hoping that the wimps would turn into Rhett Butler and carry them up the staircase. They rarely do.

Ahhh, moving right along, now. . . .

Short-term Compliance

After the trauma of initital rule-testing, you'll enter a short period of compliance. Wow, this is wonderful! You should have done this long ago. What a great book! Downing is a genius. You're happier, the house or classroom runs smoothly, and even the kids seem to like the new rules.

It seems other areas where you used to have trouble clear up. Ursula is finishing her dinner or forfeiting dessert without a fuss, and she's even going to bed without a hassle. Vera is doing her own wash or quietly wearing sink-washed damp underwear to school, and she's getting up on time, too. Little Will is saying

"Excuse me" and carrying his dishes to the sink, and he gets into his jammies when the big hand is on twelve without being asked. Amazing. You're not going to need to introduce a lot of new rules after all.

But don't give away your copy of this book to your sister-in-law with the brats just yet. There's more to come.

Milder Secondary Rule-Testing

Despite appearances, all is not well in Zion. There's got to be another session of rule-testing before all this settles out. It's called secondary rule-testing, and it is almost never as awful as initial rule-testing. Expect it, and don't give up. You've come too far to throw it all away.

Sometime soon—usually days, sometimes weeks if the rule involves an infrequent behavior like taking the trash out on Tuesday nights—the child will check in just to make sure you are really going to follow through this time.

He will "forget" the rule, manipulate you into a situation where it can't be enforced, or just grump, complain, and argue.

Here we go again, you think. I knew it wouldn't last. I knew it was too good to be true. I can't go through that again. The neighbors will think I'm abusing the child. It's just not worth it. I'll do the blasted chore myself and have some peace.

No, no, no. This is not going to be that bad. You handle it just as you did before, asking quietly without irritation, "What's the rule?" and ignoring the potential for pyrotechnics.

But usually you'll get no fireworks. Typically all you'll get is, "Oh, yeah, I forgot." Maybe you'll hear a "Scheeeez!" as he stomps off to do what he's supposed to do. Rarely will you get first-class rule-testing, and almost never will it match the original initial rule-testing.

You see, he has already accepted the rule and your authority to enforce it. Life under the rule hasn't been that bad, and in fact he's rather proud that he can be responsible. His purpose in secondary rule-testing is simply to make sure he can count on your consistency and have confidence that life is under control and predictable.

I remember a child whose rule was that he had to finish his dinner or he'd have no dessert. Sometime after the rule had been in effect, he decided that eating the limas beans was not worth the rice pudding with raisins, so he quietly excused himself and took his dishes to the kitchen. If he was expecting a hassle from his parents ("But you'll like the rice pudding. . .") he was disappointed. He had made a choice within the rule, and the parents were smart enough to ignore his quiet challenge. In spite of the overt obedience, I think we can classify this as mild secondary rule-testing.

Long-term Compliance

This is the bottom line for "Making Rules That Stick." We're looking for a situation in which the few established rules of the parent or teacher are observed without complaint, and life becomes reasonable and respectful to all concerned, caregivers *and* children.

This is the stage when people invite you and your kids to their pool and barbeque, because they know that the children will have fun but will obey the rules of the house. This is when the teacher can take the whole class outside to see the butterflies emerging from their coccoons, knowing that they'll be quiet in the hallways and won't run off across the field.

Now you can take the children to the restaurant, knowing that you won't be embarrassed. People will want their children to play with yours, hoping something will rub off. You'll bask in the envy of other parents who will wish God had given them children as fine as yours.

Teachers will smile when they see your children's names on their rolls. "Are you Xenia's sister? How nice. Fine family." They'll remember her name and unconsciously be sure she understands the lessons.

Little League coaches will appreciate how your children obey the rules of the game and are good sports when things don't go well for them.

Here's a true story. As I sit here writing, my wife has arrived with our grandson and reports that he was so good in the store the clerk asked if she could give him a Nutty-Buddy. Perfect timing. That kind of thing goes a long way to establishing wholesome self-esteem and feelings of competence.

Rule-Testing
Whenever the Environment Changes

When there are changes in the child's surroundings or routine, he goes on the alert. What else has changed? Is life still fairly predictable? What is the status of my safety, security, stability index?

How can he find out? Rule-testing.

I remember a student who had a toddler we were assured was just about perfect. "But Yensil is such a pleasant child. I really have no problem with her at all."

Fine, try one of the other projects for this course.

"Well, she does dawdle a bit over her food. I'd like her to be finished eating when my husband and I are finished."

So the mother decided that Yensil's new rule would be that she must finish her dinner by the time the adults were finished or her dinner would be removed anyway with the rest of the plates, and no dessert. Definable? Yes. Reasonable? Well, umm, I suppose, though some children are just naturally slow eaters. Enforceable? Yes. Consequence. Yes.

Each time this mother's class met, others would report, "Wow, you should have seen the initial rule-testing I got!" Or, "He's into short-term compliance, and I can't believe how much better things are."

But this family? "Nope. No rule-testing. She's fine. No dawdling. She's just an obedient child, as I said."

While the children of others in the class were

showing the predicted sequence, this paragon of virtue remained in initial compliance. My students began to roll their eyeballs at this standard report.

And then one day it happened. The mother came in subdued, and I knew she had a story. Her brother had stopped off for dinner on his way between New York and Washington. He'd never met his niece, and his sister was anxious to show her off. Such a sweet, reasonable, and obedient child.

But during dinner she was back to dawdling over her food. She stirred it around in her plate and played with it until her mother finally prompted her with, "Yensil, what's the rule about your dinner?"

The response was a sly smile and more dawdling.

I can't believe it, the mother thought. After three weeks why does she choose tonight to test the rule?

She chose tonight because there was a change in the environment, and subconsciously she needed some reassurance that her life was still stable and predictable. She also may have thought that Mother wouldn't enforce the rule with a guest at dinner. Or she may have been jealous of the attention the brother was getting and this seemed a good way to divert some in her direction.

Whatever, when the three adults finished, Mother quietly and simply took the toddler's unfinished dinner out to the kitchen with the rest of the plates. Three, not four, desserts were brought in.

"Where's my dessert? I want my dessert!"

"What's the rule about dinner and dessert, Yensil?"

"I want my dessert!" she screamed.

Mother ignored her and started eating.

More "I want my dessert!" at about 78 decibels.

"What's the rule, Yensil?"

"Bring me my dinner. I want to finish my dinner. I want my dinner and dessert!"

I think most parents would have buckled here and given her another crack at finishing the dinner. But the rule was that she had to finish her dinner by the time the adults' plates were ready to be cleared, or no dessert. She had not, so no dessert. Her mother ignored the tantrum. Pretty tough, wouldn't you say?

The child screamed, kicked, held her breath, and slid down in the high chair until she got hung up on the plastic strap in the middle and her head was hanging out the side. The father finally extracted her and banished her to her crib where she continued the tirade. The brother sat in stunned silence and I assume wondered how his sister could have raised such a brat and vowed he'd never have children of his own.

My class was delighted and breathed a collective sigh of satisfaction, and the mother became a hero in spite of her embarrassment. As I understand, she never did experience secondary rule-testing.

The point is, of course, that changes in the environment trigger rule-testing. You get your hair done differently. It's stylish and beautiful. José Eber himself would be proud. Does your husband appreciate it?

"Yeah, it's nice, I guess," he says doubtfully. And for the rest of the evening he's off his stride, shuffling around, just a little sullen. (Unconsciously: what other changes must he expect now?)

You're not well today. Sore throat, ache all over. Your children will sense the change and choose today to test all the rules.

You set the table with the pink cup at Angelica's place instead of Barbra's, who usually has it. Barbra will pound on the footrest of the high chair with her heels, push her plate away, and pour milk onto the tray. What's gotten into her? Her routine, predictable environment has changed.

There is a substitute teacher in the third grade today. This is a good class, known for their good behavior. But with the substitute they switch seats, give her wrong advice on classroom procedures, and become entirely unmanageable. The substitute teacher leaves in tears at noon and the principal spends the rest of the day with them.

Why? Are they rotten kids at heart, or are they reacting to the change of teachers? You know the answer.

A morning announcement explains that because of the assembly today, period three will meet this afternoon between periods seven and eight, and all classes will be ten minutes shorter than usual. Do you remember this? The whole school was on edge all day, and teachers were saying, "What is it with you people today?"

The environment had changed and all of this was rule-testing.

Watch for adult "rule-testing" when a new manager takes over your division, a new pastor is called to your congregation, when grandpa retires, or when your child goes through puberty.

Hints for Families Who are Moving

The average American family moves every four years. We haven't moved in a long time, so some family is doing double duty for our share. Can you think of a more disruptive experience for children, except, perhaps, moving plus a divorce? New house, new room, new neighborhood, new friends, new school, new congregation. If changes in the environment do prompt rule-testing, look out!

Years ago my wife and I decided to sell our newly built home, the only one our three children could remember, and move west for some graduate work. We packed everything in a twelve-foot trailer and waved goodbye to family and friends, house and neighborhood.

The plan was that I would drive all day while my wife tried to snooze a bit. When I got too tired at night, she would take over and I would sleep. When she got sleepy, I'd go back to the wheel and she would sleep. We'd drive all night and through the next day before stopping at a motel.

At noon she made sandwiches for all and passed out little cartons of milk. At supper time it was paper plates and beanie weenies, with chips and fruit. Fairly stable routine so far.

Finally, "Well, kids, it's eight o'clock."

"Yeah?"

"What's eight o'clock?"

Incredulously, "Jammie time?"

"Yep," she replied, and passed back each child's pajamas which she had packed in a bag by her feet.

"But we're in the car!"

"What time is it?"

"Uh, jammie time," softly.

The children washed their faces with towellettes, brushed their teeth as best they could, and had their prayers and last word. Their mother passed back each one's favorite stuffed toy, and they sat there in silence in the back seat watching trucks go by. Soon they all conked out and slept the night.

Five days pulling a trailer across the country with three kids under five? It really wasn't that bad, because we kept up some of the trappings of routine to preserve their safety, security, and stability, and they didn't have to rule test much at all.

Blending Families

If one out of every two marriages ends in divorce these days, there are a lot of single parents remarrying someone who also has a ready-made family. Disruptive to the children? Yes. Lots of rule-testing? Count on it.

I've seen enough of this to know it is a major concern in our country. I think that most of my students are either parents in a blended family or they grew up in one.

I've outlined a book on the subject, and when this manuscript gets off to the publisher, I'll flesh out the new one. If you're interested, watch for "Blending Families," or "Family Bonding," or something along those lines.

Chapter 7— Effects on Your Family:
The Environment is Changed

We've discussed at some length the effects of a few good consistently enforced rules on a child. He'll relax more, be more confident, be more obedient, and you will like him more.

What about the other children? The changed child may have been a "point man," one who has been the first to challenge authority and who has played the role of trouble maker while others watched to see his fate before sticking their own necks out.

If the point man in your family or classroom is no longer testing the limits for the others, this is a change in *their* environment. Change creates discomfort and insecurity. Rule testing results. You can expect that someone else may step forward to walk the point. You'll have to recognize what's happening and decide what steps you want to take so that you don't just exchange Tweedledum for Tweedledee.

There will be a period in which everyone is adjusting to the new circumstances.

By everyone, we have to include yourself, the caregiver. Your life is changed now, too. You're no longer in endless power struggles, no longer suffering harsh criticism from your children, no longer doing everything yourself because it's easier than getting the children to do it.

And in spite of this considerable improvement, you find yourself irritable and vaguely anxious.

Why do children of alcoholics often marry alcoholics? Why do abused spouses often marry another abuser? It's because they know what to expect from them, and in spite of the horrors they are comfortable in situations they're used to.

You may have been used to a house or classroom filled with uncontrolled kids. As dreary an existence as that was, you knew what to expect and were secure in your expectations. Now your environment has changed, and you're just a bit anxious and upset. *If you are not careful, you will unconsciously drift back into inconsistency and all the good you've accomplished will slip away.*

Protect your investment by recognizing the signs of regression in your own behavior, and don't let this happen.

I. Part Two: DISCIPLINE WITH A SMILE

Chapter 8— An Introduction to "Discipline with a Smile"

The tone of "Making Rules That Stick" has been strong and authoritarian. I believe that was necessary because so many caregivers have been beaten down and lost confidence in their ability—even their right—to control children. For a generation and more parents have been told that children should not even have rules, lest their delicate psyches be frustrated. And so in Part One of this book, I've played the role of a coach on the sidelines, shouting encouragement at the top of my lungs, urging you to remember the basics and play the game with determination. "You can do it! You're Number One!"

Now you've done it. Now the children are squared away and you're in control. And now you're ready for something even better.

Artists learn brush techniques and basic color theory before they can emerge as great masters. You've got the basics now, and you're ready to lift your family life or classroom into the joys of "Discipline with a Smile." This is icing on the cake. This is great stuff. This is fun, and both you and your children will love it. Get ready for a treat.

The Usual Results of Poor Behavior

Let's trace the typical route taken by children as they develop into misbehaving brats who drive everyone out of their skulls.

1. Child misbehaves.

2. Caregiver (parent, teacher) responds gently, "Please don't do that, dear."

3. Child continues misbehavior.

4. Caregiver escalates, "Harry, I told you not to do that."

5. Child repeats misbehavior.

6. Caregiver speaks firmly, "I'm not going to tell you again to stop that!"

7. Child continues.

8. Caregiver shouts, adding harshness, "Now you stop that right now!"

9. Child eases off, then continues with behavior.

10. Caregiver: "I've had it with you, buster! You cut that out or you're in deep doo-doo!"

11. Child backs down momentarily, then ventures forth with a slightly different form of misbehavior.

12. Caregiver: "None of that, either! Just who do you think you are? You'd better straighten out or you'll wish you had!"

Notice that at this point whatever else was occupying the attention of the family or class has long been forgotten, as child and caregiver take center stage in the drama of a power struggle.

Much Ado but Little Done

If it's a school situtation, the child may be sent to the office for handling by the professional hatchet-person there. Chances are he'll get to sit in a chair near the big glass hallway windows as he waits for the executioner. Friends will walk by and laugh with him or call in messages of encouragement. Maybe even the little red-haired girl will see him and realize that he's bigtime, not just some weasely classroom irritant.

After "a good talking to" at the office, the child will be sent back to his classroom and disrupt the lesson again as he swaggers and grins and snorts to his seat.

Does behavior change? Not really. Tomorrow is more of the same. Someday soon the vice-principal will decide to schedule an interview for him with the guidance counselor.

After two or three such interviews—but little change in behavior—the guidance counselor will ask for a meeting of the Child Study Team. That will take place next Thursday, because members of the team have a full load of other cases and duties.

At the meeting of the Child Study Team (which consists of the classroom teacher, the guidance counselor, the vice-principal, the school nurse, and the school psychologist), it will be decided that a meeting should be held with Harry's parents. A letter will be written and sent. Dates and schedules will be juggled.

The child's father is not available for such a meeting, but his mother will arrive and sit nervously at the end of the table. All but she will have a folder and important looking papers in front of them.

"We're concerned with Harry's behavior, Mrs. Horsechester. I wonder if you could shed a little light on it." Implicit in the tone is that the child's behavior is rooted in the home and the school is suffering because of the parent's failure.

"Well, ever since [whatever], he's become more and more difficult to handle, and I've reached the point where I just don't know what to do with him. He doesn't pay any attention to anything I say." Cleverly, the parent has expressed defeat and shifted reponsibility for fixing the child back to the school.

The members of the Child Study Team really don't have any answers, but it seems a shame to wrap up the meeting so quickly. What follows is a litany of the boy's crimes with everyone at the table adding their own horror stories and participating with knowing nods and sympathetic shakes of the head.

Finally it will be decided that the school psychologist should have a go at him to uncover the deep rooted causes of his disruptive behavior. Everyone will smile with relief and go back to their comfortable routines.

Of course, there's only one school psychologist, and Harry can't be scheduled right away. Early April is about the best we can do. Meantime, Harry will continue in classes.

Once a week for four weeks in April, Harry will spend thirty minutes telling the psychologist what he wants him to hear. It's neat getting out of class occasionally and having an adult devote his entire attention to him for half an hour. The best he's been able to get out of his teacher has been fifteen to twenty minutes, but of course, he has a larger audience in the classroom and that compensates somewhat.

By the end of April the psychologist's report will be ready: Harry has deep-seated problems stemming from the traumas of childhood and would probably benefit from regular therapy. The parent will be advised to consider "getting him into counseling." The teacher will be advised that since the school year is almost over, she should endure until the boy moves on to another teacher who may have more success with him.

What has changed? Nothing, really, except that the caregiving establishment has eased its conscience by holding meetings, conducting studies, and writing reports.

Much ado but little done.

Chapter 9— Some Alternatives to the Caregiver in Handling Any Behavior

What is a parent or teacher or school to do? We can't let the inmates take over the asylum. Truth be told, though, that's exactly what's happened in thousands of homes and schools.

There was a day when "incorrigible children" were placed in reform schools or orphanages. In our more enlightened society, however, we offer group homes in a residential setting. Behavior may not change much, but at least the professional caregivers get some time off to refresh their sanity, a blessing most harried parents don't have. In really tough cases, lithium and Prozac may be brought in to help manage the incarcerated child's behavior.

But except in very extreme cases, we can't simply expel the troublemakers from school anymore. School today is not a privilege earned by cooperative behavior. Many states have laws guaranteeing children "the right to a thorough and efficient education" until age sixteen.

Since some children are beyond management at a regular school, we see little minibuses ferrying children to alternative schools designed to contain their behavior.

They're often in the same vehicles with innocent children who have special physical, neurological, or emotional needs. In fact, to gain funding for dealing with troublemakers, we often classify them as emotionally disturbed when they are really just disruptive children who haven't learned acceptable behavior.

Punishment

Historically, society has relied upon punishment. The "hickory stick" was a standard item of issue to parents and teachers. The humiliating dunce cap stood nearby. At home it was "to bed without supper," "go-to-your-room," or "grounding."

Advantages of Punishment

Punishment does work. It does seem to stop the misbehavior, at least momentarily. It does acknowledge the caregiver's authority, at least publically. It does let the world know that the caregiver is "not a wimp," saving some face among friends. It does let the caregiver vent his/her frustration, which Freudian cardiologists might think is healthy.

Disadvantages of Punishment

The problem is that punishment doesn't work very well nor do its effects last very long.

I know, I can hear the cries of protest from here. Once when you were a child you took something from the store and your mother marched you right back and made you apologize and you've never stolen anything since. Yes, there are some instances where punishment has had a lasting impact.

But for the most part, if punishment were so effecive, why do punished children continue to misbehave? The world should be full of pleasant dutiful children. Is this the world you walk in? It's not like that in my mall.

I'll wager that for every instance of effective punishment, you can think of a hundred where the child went back to the misbehavior even after being punished.

Punishment is often associated with the source. If a child is taught to be afraid of a punishment, it's natural that he might generalize to become afraid of the source of the punishment. "Just wait 'til your father comes home!" does little for father/child relationships. But even if each parent handles his/her own punishments, where is the value in being associated with such unpleasantness?

One reason punishment doesn't last is that it's unpleasant, and people try to forget unpleasant things. Psychologists call it *repression* when the forgetting just happens and *suppression* when we try to forget. Either way, it's forgotten.

Freud, however, believed it wasn't really gone but remained lurking in the unconscious to make us anxious or to effect our behavior in ways we can't understand.

For example, a child punished by being thrust into a dark closet may not remember that punishment in later life. But he could have a fear of closed places (claustrophobia) and not know why. Another threatened by the "boogieman" may have forgotten the threats but find himself unaccountably tense in the presense of men who resemble his fantasy. ("He's b-i-i-g and his face is bl-a-a-ck. . .") Is this a cause of the irrational fear and prejudice some people carry all their lives?

Putting Freud aside, what is the value of a punishment if the mind tries to forget it? We need a discipline technique that will last a long time. Stay with us.

Why Punishment Continues Anyway

But if punishment is so ineffective, why do we caregivers continue using it? There are several reasons. Can you spot the ones that apply in your situation?

Punishment May Really be Reward

What is punishing to you may not be punishing to the child. Tom Sawyer took Becky Thatcher's whipping by confessing to her crime. "The surprise, the gratitude, the adoration that shone upon him out of poor Becky's eyes seemed pay enough for a hundred floggings."

A teacher's criticism may be rewarding to a child who is hoping to be one of the gang by tantalizing teachers. "Wow!" the other kids marvel. "Did you see the vein standing out on her forehead? I thought she was going to have a stroke when you said, 'Who, me?'" Thank you, thank you. Tune in tomorrow for my next act.

I recall a principal's lecture about the ten percent of the student body who ruin it for the rest. Soon there was an informal club of the "Ten Percenters." Perhaps they went on to join the Warlocks, a local motorcycle gang around here who sported "1%'er" tatoos.

Look at the usual detention hall in a high school. The detendees are often regulars who vie for having the most detentions yet to serve. It's become a social thing to them.

"Where were you last night?"

"Oh, I had to get off for a dentist's appointment, but I'll be back today."

They may as well elect officers and have a photo taken for the yearbook.

As a public school teacher I handled my own discipline problems. I used negative reinforcement in my own detention in my own classroom. More on negative reinforcement later. It's not punishment, by the way.

I remember one student who became a regular in my detention. He seemed to be just a kid who had a hard time keeping from making snide remarks about everything that went on in class, and I was working on teaching him control over his extraneous comments. But every day he was back. He was still with me long after the other infractors had gone home. He just couldn't sit quietly.

And then it hit me. He *enjoyed* my detentions. I was likely the only one in the school—teachers or students—who spoke to him quietly and with dignity and respect for him. His time with me after school was a reward, and he got it by disobeying my prime rule, "No talking while the teacher is talking." I was reinforcing his poor behavior.

The solution? I told the boy that I hoped I could continue as his friend and that he was welcome to stop around after school to say hello, but since I just couldn't handle him in the classroom I was trading him to another teacher for two of her most difficult students. (She was a screamer and he knew it.) He pled for one last chance and shaped up.

Here's a common home effort. The parent gets tough and passes sentence, "You go to your room and stay there for thirty minutes!"

Yes, that's punishment if the child is involved in something he is enjoying. It's not punishment if he's into something he hates, like raking the leaves with his little brother, or being bored to death on a rainy afternoon with his sister.

It's punishment if the room is dull and uninteresting. It's not punishment if it's cool and quiet and has his favorite books, magazines, models, tape deck, TV and computer.

A child who creeps halfway down the stairs during his parents' party is not punished when his parents reprimand him loudly, allowing the audience to focus on how cute he can be in his pajamas. He may even sense

DISCIPLINE WITH A SMILE

how proud they are of him. "My, he's grown so big!" their guests acknowledge. Thank you, thank you. I'll be down for my second act later.

Here's a quote from the father of a child in for counseling. "That's the seventh time I've had to spank him today, but he still doesn't listen. He's just like I was. He's got a mind of his own." That's a virtue in some circles, and the child could almost hear the admiration in the father's voice.

Perversely, there are a few children who seek out punishment to ease the guilt for some perceived sin. They may have ruined Mother's career by being born. They may feel they are the cause of their parents' divorce. They may have survived when their brother was drowned. They may be whole while their sister is handicapped. They may have been playing "doctor" with a little friend and surely God will punish them with some dread disease or by sending them to hell. But if they accumulate enough punishment, perhaps God will feel they've suffered enough and spare them.

Modeling

Some parents persist in punishing because they learned how to parent by watching their own parents, and that's all they know. They vowed they'd never treat their children the way they were treated, but now as parents of unruly kids they slide right into the role of harsh parent. "Good grief," they catch themselves. "I sound just like my mother."

Power

It's a heady thing to have authority. Do this, do that, and they have to do it, ha, ha, ha. Wow!

"Nobody's ever paid any attention to me all my life, but you'd better believe my children are going to listen!"

"Because *I* said so, that's why."

"Sit up straight! Fold your hands on your desk! Put both feet on the floor! Get rid of that gum! This is the worst class I've ever had!" What a power kick!

Some teachers will even unconsciously single out some poor hapless child for special persecution. Why? Because the child resembles a hated classmate from years ago who persecuted the future teacher.

Learned Behavior

Now we're going to get a little sophisticated and introduce a psychological principle.

That behavior which is most closely associated with a desired outcome becomes a conditioned behavior and tends to be repeated.

This is very important and we will use it throughout the rest of this book. But for now, let's see how it works in causing caregivers to continue using punishment even when punishment clearly is not working well.

Example: Ms. Ararat is trying to stop the undertone of talking during her lecture.

"Class, I want it quiet in here."

119

It gets quiet and she continues her presentation. One minute later the mumbling has risen again.

"Class, I said quiet!" she says with irritation.

It gets quiet and she continues her presentation. One minute later they're at it again.

"Will. . .you. . .please. . .settle. . .*down!*"

It gets quiet and she continues her presentation. One minute later it's as bad as ever.

"All right, class, SHUT UP!!"

It gets quiet and she continues her presentation. But in another minute it's as if she'd never spoken.

Is her shouting and harshness working? Obviously not. But she's an intelligent woman. Why does she continue to use this ineffective strategy?

The answer is that she has been conditioned to do so by the principle of association: *That behavior which is most closely associated with a desired outcome becomes a conditioned behavior and tends to be repeated.*

What does she want? Quiet.

When does she get it? When she harranges and shouts and screams. The quiet is most closely associated with her use of a punishing tone and language.

The poor behavior—the undertone in the background—rises a little later and is not as closely associated with her screaming as is the sudden quiet, so she has been conditioned—taught, trained—to use punishment. She becomes known as a screamer, and other teachers will sigh heavily and close their classroom doors.

If parents want children to do what they ask, they may start out kindly. "Billy, remember to hang up your coat."

No response.

"Billy, hang your coat up."

Nothing.

"Billy, you hang that coat up or I'm gonna whack you up alongside the head!"

Billy hangs up his coat.

What is most closely associated with coat hanging behavior? Harshness.

What kind of discipline is the parent being conditioned to use? Harshness.

Parenthetically, what does the child associate most closely with having to hang up his coat? The harsh tone of the parent. Then, to what kind of discipline has *he* become conditioned to respond? The harsh tone of the parent, not the original mild reminder. They're co-conditioned, actors going through their lines, repeating the same show every day.

Real quick now, how can we condition Billy to hang up his coat when he comes in the door instead of waiting for a hassle from his parent? Let's go back to the principle of association: *That behavior which is most closely associated with a desired outcome becomes a conditioned behavior and tends to be repeated.*

What is our desired outcome? Billy will hang up his coat.

What can we place closest to his coat hanging behavior? His coming in the door.

Try this. Billy comes in the door and tosses his coat on the couch. In the past you have shouted, "Hang that coat up, muttonhead!"

This time, you say, "Billy, you missed something. Put your coat on, go outside, and come back in and see if you can get it right."

He grumbles that he'll hang it up now, but no, you want his coat hanging to become associated with coming in the door, so you insist he put it on again and go out.

Every time he forgets, it's coat on, back outside, come in again, hang up coat. Soon he is conditioned to hang the coat up when he comes in instead of being conditioned to hang it up when you shout at him. In fact, you may never have to mention it again.

Nevertheless, there's an even better way to condition Billy to hang up coats, take out trash, not hit his sister, etc. That's coming up soon, but first, we need to understand ignoring.

Ignoring

Ignoring is the principle of benign neglect. It's very effective and easy to learn. Unfortunately, it's hard to convince caregivers that it really works until they try it.

Your mother couldn't convince you that it works when you were a child and the other kids were calling you by a hated nickname.

Remember, she said, "Don't pay any attention to them and they'll stop"?

"No they won't!" you cried, and continued to get upset and stalk off or tell the teacher. And they continued to whisper it in class and shout it on the playground.

Mother was right. (The best psychologist is an intelligent, thoughtful mother.) In the profession the principle reads like this:

That which is reinforced tends to be repeated. That which is not reinforced (ignored) tends to be extinguished.

I remember teaching this principle once, and after class a student came up and asked if this works with adults. Oh, yes. It does.

He said he was a waiter, and the chef had a disgusting nickname for him which was spreading throughout the restaurant. He had talked to him, pleaded with him, threatened him. Nothing stopped it. I encouraged him to try ignoring it—non-reinforcement.

That night he went to the chef and told him, "My name is Chuck. From now on I'm not going to respond to anything else. You want to talk to me, you use my right name." And he walked away.

Of course, the chef tried the nickname. But there was no response. No anger, no stalking off, no repeating of the decision. He was ignored—not reinforced for using the tantalizing nickname, "Upchuck." It was over in an hour and the nickname never used again.

When children misbehave, they are often reinforced by our distress and attention, so the behavior continues. If we can manage to ignore it, the behavior usually extinguishes, that is, it goes away.

Here's a classic story for you. Donny was the worst child in the third grade. He occupied more of his teacher's attention than the rest of the class combined. He was out of his seat most of the time, disturbed the other children, started fights, broke into lines, and had made practically no progress on his schoolwork. His teacher was ready to leave the profession, and it was only October.

A specialist in behavior modification was called in to observe the class. The first sight he had of Donny was of him jumping off the piano and shouting, "Geronimo!"

Soon the specialist discovered that the children were "helping" the teacher by tattling on Donny.

"Donny pushed in front of the line again."

The teacher responded with, "Thank you, Eva. Donny, you get back in your place. Right now. Go on."

"Donny punched me on the arm!"

"Are you all right, Fran? Did it make a bruise? Donny, if you can't stop hitting people, I'm going to have to send you down to the principal's office again. Is that what you want? Is it? Do you want people to go around afraid of you all the time."

Do you see what was happening? Donny was being reinforced (rewarded) with attention, even though the teacher thought she was punishing him with her disapproval.

And more: the students were being reinforced with attention by reporting Donny's misbehavior. Might they have been provoking some of it? Could this have been a subliminal game in which all players were getting a payoff?

The payoff—the reinforcement, the reward—was attention. The partial solution? Withdraw the attention from the students when they tattled, making Donny's behavior merely tiresome to them instead of the source of getting attention for the tattler.

Now, there's more in Donny's case, and we'll pick him up again a little later on. Ignoring alone is not enough, but it *is* critical to success in changing poor behavior.

Advantages of Ignoring Poor Behavior

The advantage to ignoring poor behavior is that it's easy enough to do. No training, no complex ideas. You just simply ignore the poor behavior. We discussed this earlier in "Making Rules that Stick." You don't react. You don't sigh heavily, nor roll your eyeballs to heaven, nor stalk out of the room. You just ignore it.

Now, there *are* some caveats—things to watch out for. Read on.

What must be added to enhance advantages

You may ignore the poor behavior. But what if you're living with other people in the household?

For example, suppose you're living with your in-laws. You can ignore poor behavior, but if it gets a rise out of Grandma it's not being ignored. You've got to enlist her in the effort, which may be difficult because she has her own agenda.

She may want you to fail with the child so that you can share in the frustration she felt years ago with his father.

She may want you to fail because she will then be proven superior to your new-fangled ideas.

She may want you to fail because she hates you for taking her favorite son away from her. If the father is intimidated by her and won't stand with you on this, you've got more problems than just the child.

You've either got to get your own place or make her part of your team to bring this kid under control. She's got to learn how to ignore poor behavior.

Even if you're in your own home you've got others to consider. It's been said that you get to raise only one child: your first. Your second child is raised by you, your spouse and the first child. The third child is raised by you, your spouse, and the first two children.

You may decide, "We will ignore his tantrum." You may, but what about the other children?

Disadvantages of Ignoring Poor Behavior

There are disadvantages to ignoring poor behavior. You'll discover this at the mall, with hundreds of people watching you and shaking their heads while you don't respond to the child's whining for a new toy.

A second disadvantage is that it doesn't work immediately. The child actually has to misbehave and get no response a few times before his previously conditioned behavior becomes extinguished. This can be wearing and a nuisance.

A third disadvantage to ignoring poor behavior is that there may be some inherent reinforcement in the behavior itself. You can ignore the child stealing cookies from the cookie jar all you please, but the cookies themselves are reinforcing.

You can stand aside and not acknowledge his marking grafitti on the wall, but there's a satisfaction in getting the curve in the "S" just right that is rewarding to the child.

Or, the shocked reaction of the recipient of your child's obscene phone call is something beyond your control.

By the way, the best advice in handling nuisance calls is simply to hang up. No response. No gasps nor clever comebacks, no whistles into the mouthpiece, no threats or expressions of disgust. Ignore them. They will stop. *That which is ignored tends to be extinguished.*

What Must be Done to Overcome the Disadvantages of Ignoring

If you're very creative or clever you can find a way to remove inherent reinforcement from many poor behaviors.

As a small boy I thought it great fun to imprint my name on wet cement or to carve it on tree trunks. And my wise father chose not to hassle me for deeds that could not be undone. But I distinctly remember a day on the tower at Valley Forge when we came across some kids' names painted on the guard panels.

"Fools' names and fools' faces, always seen in public places," he intoned. Simple enough, but it had the effect of taking the pleasure out of having my name plastered around where it shouldn't be. Is that what people thought when they saw my art work? He had removed the reinforcement.

He did the same by anthropomorphizing trees. "See how the sap has oozed out of the wound in the bark caused by some tenderfoot's knife." Poor tree. Thoughtless kid.

How's this one? "After nose rings go out of style, do you think that hole in that girl's nose will heal up or leave a pock mark?" No outrage, no validation of rising generation rebellion—just a quiet contemplation of a negative to offset the pleasure.

My own interest in owning a Corvette faded when my son-in-law called it a selfish man's car. No room for your friends, he observed. Hmmm. Go for the Jag.

Somehow, if you can, try to devise a way to remove inherent positive reinforcement in undersirable behavior. Just ignoring behavior doesn't always do the job.

Negative reinforcement

Here is an excellent technique of behavior modification—negative reinforcement. Many people misunderstand negative reinforcement. They think it's punishment, and it's not.

Negative reinforcement is when you put the child in an unpleasant situation, and when he behaves the way you want him to, you release him.

When I was a child there was a dreadful "joke" going around that went, "Did you hear about the moron who pounded his head with a hammer because it felt so good when he stopped?"

Well, negative reinforcement is something like that. It feels so good to the child when he gets out of it.

Negative reinforcement is powerful. It's not as strong as positive reinforcement (coming up), but it's a lot better than punishment.

If your child misbehaves and you send him to his room *for thirty minutes*, that's punishment.

If he misbehaves and you send him to his room *until* he acts like a reasonable human being, that's negative reinforcement.

As a public school teacher I ran my own detention hall. The one operated by the principal was planned as punishment (which doesn't work well) but more probably was reward, a period of comraderie among miscreants.

I had few but very carefully enforced rules in my classroom. "No one talks while the teacher is talking," is the one which tripped up most rule testers. As a result, for the first few days of school I'd have a room full of detentionees.

It was pitiful. There was the usual assortment of "bad kids" who counted it a day lost when they hadn't driven some teacher to tears. But there would also be a few sweet young things who had been charming teachers all their lives and had never had a dee-tent-shun. Close to tears, they'd sit with eyes down and pounding pulses.

I'd call the session to order. "Thank you for coming today. As you know, this activity is for people who find it hard to be quiet. We shall practice being quiet. The quieter it is, the shorter it is."

Then I'd sit at my desk and grade papers. After three or four minutes, I'd notice one or two students who had been absolutely quiet. "Okay, George, you can go. Thanks for coming in."

"Hey, where's he goin'?"

"The quieter it is, the shorter it is."

"I ain't gonna sit around here all day. I gotta get to work."

"The quieter it is, the shorter it is."

After a minute or so more, I'd excuse two or three more quiet students. "Thanks for coming in." No hassles about better behavior next time. They were released from the unpleasant detention as soon as they showed the desired behavior. Negative reinforcement.

"What's this! I want to get out of here someday. How long do we have to stay?"

"The quieter it is, the shorter it is." No criticism, no lectures.

You could see the wheels starting to spin in their heads. Suddenly even the loudest mouth was quiet, with hands folded on desk, in case I hadn't noticed.

"Okay, Harry, you can go, too. Thanks for coming in." Zoom, and he was gone, without even questioning my curious courtesy. My detentions rarely lasted more than fifteen or twenty minutes, and after three weeks I'd only have one or two clients a day.

Oh, you protest, but they weren't really sorry. Their behavior was just a show so they'd get out quickly.

I know. That's okay. And a few will break the rule again tomorrow. But children do learn the required behavior regardless of their sincerity. Some learn it sooner, and a few learn it later. But negative reinforcement works very nicely, thank you.

Try it at home. Instead of sending the child to his room for thirty minutes, send him to his room until he calms down and can talk with you quietly. He'll be out in five minutes, and you'll be able to reason with him. If not, send him back until he's ready.

Do you remember your son playing kicksoccer in the side yard, who when losing would start hassling the other kids and acting like a poor sport? When you called him in and sent him to his room, you were getting him out of an unpleasant situation, i.e., the losing game and the danger of him embarrassing himself by bursting into tears. Without realizing it, you were using negative reinforcement to strengthen his poor sportsmanlike behavior.

And if his room were cool and quiet, filled with interesting things to do and look at, you were actually rewarding him for his poor sportsmanship, adding positive reinforcement to negative reinforcement. You couldn't have designed a more powerful technique to strengthen his poor behavior.

In one Maryland reformatory, they used positive

reinforcement using a token economy. But they coupled this with negative reinforcement by taking kids who were "acting out" (a euphamism for violent behavior) and thrusting them into a dull room with no window, gray painted walls, and a single light bulb hanging from the ceiling.

This might have been punishment, but they would watch the kid through a peephole while he flung himself around the room shouting obsenities. When he finally exhausted himself and slumped down to sit on the floor and lean against the wall, they'd call in.

"Ira. . .You okay?"

Pause. "Yeah."

"Got yourself under control?"

"Yeah."

"Want to come out to the land of the living?"

"Yeah!"

"Fine, here you go. The guys are playing pool. Why don't you watch until the next game?"

This combination of positive and negative reinforcement was so powerful that hardened delinquents responded and were turned around. From 70% recidivism to 30% recidivism. Great stuff.

Hold it, though. There was a school for retarded boys in Philadelphia where the staff had heard about the success in the Maryland reformatory.

"Hmmm. We don't have an extra room we can use for a 'time-out room.' Let's see. . .we'll use a foot locker." Argh! (Those involved were fired.)

Chapter 10—Positive Reinforcement: The Crowning Jewel of Behavior Modification

Now we've come to the heart of this book. This is the pot of gold you've been trudging toward over the past many pages. With your skills in consistency honed to a fine edge, with your hapless reliance on punishment brought into question, you're ready to change your life.

You are about to be transformed from the warden of the jail to the giver of all good things. You're going to trade in your ogre's costume for a Santa Claus suit. You'll no longer be the object of resentment but the recipient of sincere gratitude. And it's very possible this will happen overnight.

You will love this technique. Your children will love it with you. Your friends will marvel at the pleasant atmosphere in your home, and your in-laws will praise your obedient children. Teachers who try this will find their students highly motivated and well behaved.

No, it's not too good to be true. I see it happen all the time. And when it doesn't happen, the variable seems not to be the children involved but how well the caregivers follow the outline below.

The material that follows is really critical. More than twenty-five years of the experiences of many parents and teachers have brought us to this highly refined procedure. Follow it carefully and succeed, or skim it and fail.

Rewards

Rewards are the key to changing behavior easily, quickly, and if done right, permanently.

What's this? Do I detect a jaundiced scepticism? Consider: rewards are the key to the free enterprise system of prosperity, which with all its faults has resulted in the highest standard of living in the history of the world.

Altruism is an exalted concept, but it failed the USSR. They're not our allies now because they love peace. They are allies because they're broke. In spite of altruism, adopted by a few and forced upon many, the richest region in the world still imports grain.

Rewards are an eternal principle. It's the Law of the Harvest. As a man sows, thus doth he reap. As I write this I can see the scraggly little tomato plants in my little garden. Last evening I visited with a friend while he irrigated his plot, filled with vibrant tomatoes, plump onions, healthy potatoes, and vigorous corn. I worked little and will reap little. He learned how it's done and did it, and he'll have his pantry filled for the winter.

Walt Disney had a cartoon out fifty years ago called "The Grasshopper and the Ants." The grasshopper filled his summer days by strumming and singing, "Oh, the world owes me a living. . ." The ants, as you can guess, spent their time doing worthwhile things and had enough for the winter. The grasshopper died.

I haven't seen that cartoon for years. In fact, I haven't heard that concept for years. When was it that we stopped teaching children that their present behavior has an immutable effect on their future circumstances?

Was it when religion became unpopular?

Dear God, We Miss You

Most of you parents and teachers who are reading this book don't remember when it was okay to express religious beliefs in public.

Back then, Hollywood offered the country films such as Bing Crosby in "The Bells of St. Mary's," when priests were shown as pastors of the poor rather than perverted pedophiles.

Hokey though some of those films may have been, they reflected society's belief that good actions were rewarded by good consequences.

There were grand epics such as *"The Robe," "Quo Vadis,"* and *"The Ten Commandments."* In the latter, producer Cecil B. DeMille introduced the film with a prologue—"We cannot break the Ten Commandments. We can only break ourselves against them."

The last significant acknowledgement in films showing religion as respectable may have been with *"Ben Hur"*: God rewards the patient and the humble in his own due time and way.

I don't remember my parents ever going to church. But when I was a boy growing up in the lean days of the Great Depression and World War II, I was sent every

Sunday to the little brick church up the street. Many of my classmates attended a white frame Baptist Church on the other side of town, and some went up the pike to Our Lady, Queen of Peace.

A few of my friends didn't attend any church, but that didn't matter much. We all believed in God and that shaped our behavior to some extent.

For example, when I succumbed to childish envy and pocketed one of Jerry's little toy trucks, it weighed heavily in my pants all the way home. I hid it for a couple of days, but I knew that I had stolen and I knew that God knew it. Finally I slipped it back in my little friend's box of toys, and probably he never realized it had been gone.

As an adolescent there were the same temptations teens face today. It might have been a little harder to sin then, but a clever fellow could find a way to do most everything if he had a mind to. Parents could be manipulated then as now, teachers could be outsmarted, and the police didn't know the neighborhood as thoroughly as we did.

But even after I stopped going to church, God was still there, and "angels above us were silent notes taking." We did risk some things, but we hoped for enough time left in life to repent and get straightened out before that great Final Exam in the Sky.

And Exam there would be. Everyone knew that. Every light-fingered little boy, every drunken father, every wayward girl earning popularity with her body knew that. We all knew that the day would come when a white-bearded Father on a golden throne would sit in judgment of us and we would have a bright recollection of all our guilt.

No more. God has been banished from everyday life. He's been dropped from polite conversation for many years, expelled from the schools, and generally relegated to the status of a homeless old geezer on the streets whose eye no one meets and who has been passed over by a more affluent generation.

The direct results? The little boys see a better future in dealing drugs than attending school. *Philadelphia Magazine* quotes a little girl, "I was going to save myself until I was twelve, but then I fell in love." In some areas young men gain status by having fathered two or three babies in the neighborhood. Couples looking to marriage worry about contracting AIDS from their fiancés. "Fatal attractions" introduce dreaded diseases to faithful partners. Innocent children are badly abused. Fifty percent of marriages break up on whims or through no comprehension of responsibility. Bankers take the money and run, and politicians are strangers to the truth. The media take advantage of a man for his words, and industries mask their ingredients and pollutants.

If you're clever enough to avoid the law, no one can do a thing. Victims are prosecuted for using undue force, and the grisly murderer has advocates meeting in candlelight vigil to save him from "cruel and unusual punishment." Thrill seekers shoot randomly at a group on the corner, and then check the paper in the morning to see who they killed.

DISCIPLINE WITH A SMILE

The courts have protected us from the tyranny of a government sponsored church. "But when they are learned they think they are wise," and their lack of wisdom has robbed us of the glue that gave us order.

God had protected us from much of this. Or, at least, our acknowledgement of the existance of a God who would hold us accountable for our actions protected us. A belief in a note-taking God is crucial to a safe and stable society.

Dear God, wherever you are, we miss you.

Behavior Modification
through Positive Reinforcement

Can parents and caregivers, in the face of a world rooted in the pleasures of the present, hope to teach children that good behavior pays off in the future? I think we can, and I think a system of rewards—behavior modification through positive reinforcement—can help us.

What is truly rewarding?

Rewards work. They work so well it's frightening. They work even when we don't realize what is going on. What we discussed above under "Punishment—Why Punishment Can Really Be Reward" holds true here.

For example, you tell Greta that if she finishes her liver and onions she can have a second helping of broccoli. Won't work? But *you* love broccoli. Doesn't everyone?

We need to find out what is truly rewarding to the child in order for the reward to be effective.

If Heathcliff finishes weeding the flower bed he can go to the party. That's fine if Heathcliff *wants* to go to the party. But suppose he feels inferior to the other party goers and hates them but doesn't want to admit it. You've chosen the wrong reward. It won't work.

You praise Ira for his good penmanship. "You're not like some others in this class who are sloppy and won't take the time to be neat."

But if those others are his friends, the praise is not rewarding. He'll have to find something fast to bring down criticism upon him and square himself with his pals. Your "reward" didn't work because it wasn't really rewarding.

Real rewards do work. They work well and they work fast. You respond to rewards. You get up and go to work when you'd rather stay in bed, because you want the reward of the paycheck or promotion or prestige.

You wear certain clothing because you enjoy the reward of occasional compliments. You leave other items in the closet because they get no response (they're ignored), and you've begun to wonder if they look bad on you.

You cook certain meals for your family because you get praised for them. Or you work hard in the yard because people notice the results and approve.

You'll uproot your family and move across the continent because the boss has "sweetened the deal" and made you an offer you really can't refuse. Rewards.

Does this mean we believe that every man has his price? Well, sort of. *"Indecent Proposal"* was a sorry example of that. But even if you say, "Never, not me," you may be saying that maintaining your honor is more important than whatever else is being offered as a reward. Respect, dignity and honor are vastly underestimated as rewards, a concept that many caregivers have not understood.

We need to find out what the *child* sees as rewarding. A little further on we're going to ask you go to the source—to find out by sitting down with the child and asking him.

Respect as Reward

What might your children find rewarding? You'll probably think of the obvious ones first: a new bike, a new computer game, an excursion to Chucky Cheese. But we miss out when we neglect respect, dignity, and honor. Try some of the following phrases on your children and watch their reactions.

"Did I give you too many beans, Jared?" (I respect your tastes even though I want you to eat vegetables.)

"Would you like your dessert now, or do you want to go out and play for a while and then have it when it's time to come in?" (I respect your freedom generally.)

"It sounds like school has become a bit of a drag for you recently. What can I do to help?" (I care about you and am willing to take my time for you.)

Respect as Reward

"Would you like to show me your homework before you turn it in so that I can help you with the rough spots?" (I don't want your dignity to be damaged by your turning in poor work.)

"Would you mind bringing in the trash barrels from the curb as soon as you come home from school. They look ugly in front of the house." (Courtesy and respect in "would you mind"; dignity and honor in concern for the neighborhood.)

Can you get a feel for the flavor of the above? Would you have responded well to such comments by your parents? Do you wish your own supervisor would realize how pleasant (rewarding) it is to be spoken to in such tones?

Notice how important this is on the street: "Hey, you dissin' me, man?" Are you being disrespectful? I've worked in tough neighborhoods as an insurance investigator and with kids in juvenile detention centers. The key to being effective is to grant people—children included—their innate right to dignity.

Perhaps you can't respect them. Their life style is repugnant to you. Maybe you can't honor them for anything they've done. But they're all human beings and for that quality alone they deserve dignity.

You say, "please" and "thank you." You say, "Would you mind [whatever]," or "I'd appreciate it if you would [fill in the blank]." This offers a rare and prized dignity to people who don't get much of it. It is intensely rewarding to them, and children—almost everyone—will respond with the behavior you've asked for. It is not weak. It *is* effective.

141

Esteem as Behavior Modification

Brigham Young University produced a film years ago called "Johnny Lingo." I insist that all of my child and educational psychology students see it. It's stylized—almost a sociodrama—not a vehicle for method actors. Its enduring popularity over twenty-five years is in its simplicity. (It's still available. Write for it.)

Johnny Lingo is the sharpest trader in all the islands. He could have any girl he choses. For a typical wife he must pay a bride price of three cows to her father. Four cows brings a superior one. Johnny chooses pitiful Mahana.

On the day of bargaining Mahana hides in a tree. "Mahana, you ugly," her father calls. "Do you want me to come up there and put bruises all over you so that Johnny Lingo will see what a disobedient daughter you are?"

The crowd from the village gathers. "One cow is all he can ask," they speculate. "If Moki asks for two cows, Johnny Lingo will settle for one."

Moki confides, "If he offered me a cow that gave sour milk, I would accept it gratefully."

In the bargaining, Moki asks for three. Johnny counters with eight. Eight? The village is amazed.

"Never in the history of our island has anyone paid eight cows for a wife. And for Mahana?"

A few months later the newlyweds return after an extensive honeymoon and trading journey. Mahana is radiant. "Is it her? She's gracious and beautiful! She's worth ten cows if she's worth a hoof!"

What made the difference? "It was the cows. In her father's hut she thought she was worth nothing. Now she knows she is worth more than any woman on the island...I wanted her to *be* an eight cow woman."

Hokey? Well, sure, but my married students wonder if I might offer another screening just for husbands.

People become what we think of them. No, that's not quite right. People become what *they* think we think of them. You've heard of the fellow who at his wife's funeral remarked how much he had loved her, and "I almost told her once, too."

What do our children think we think of them?

If they think we think they're sneaky, they become sneaky. But if they think we think they're trustworthy, they become trustworthy.

If they think we think they're lazy, they act lazy. If they think we think they try hard, they do try hard.

Have you seen the *Homefront Spots* on TV:

"Hey, Dad, I'm almost done my model."

"Well, don't forget to clean up. You know how messy you are."

Or, "Madilyn, I told you I was going to wash those jeans. Sometimes you're so dense."

There's more: "Give your sister some. Why do you have to be so stingy?"

Child running into the house: "Dad, Dad, I got two 'A's!"

"How many times do I have to tell you not to slam the door!"

A child becomes what he thinks we think of him.

"Say, you're almost done with your model. You sure are good with your hands."

"Two 'A's? That's great! Come on up and let's have a look at them!"

"I like the way you fixed your room. You have a real sense of neatness."

"Everything is hard at first, but I know you can do it. It's good the way you stick at things even when you get discouraged."

"You keep getting grades like this and your teacher is going to want to have all our children in her class."

Of course, though, you've got to be sincere. Kids aren't stupid. They know when you're trying to con them, and that's not only dishonest, it's ineffective. But you can find something good to say about almost anything.

"Say, you've chosen mighty pretty colors for your scrib. . .uh, drawing."

"Well, that's a different hair style. Did you design it yourself?"

Who was the politician who gasped at the homliest infant he'd ever been asked to kiss and gushed, "Now there's a *baby!*"

Signals of Approval

We really don't have to gush. We communicate more by body language anyway. We just have to be sure that the message sent is the message received.

Simple Attention

Non-verbal communication is very effective in the classroom, as well as at home. A smile with eye contact. A knowing glance. A nod, or simply paying attention to the child. We underestimate the impact of such simple reinforcers.

There's an urban legend in academia of a psychology professor who had lectured her last class on the theories of *shaping* as taught by B.F. Skinner. When she was late for the next session her students agreed among themselves that they would pay attention only when she lectured from the left side of the room.

So, while she spoke from the left side, they were all interest and attention. When she paced to the right, it was boredom and woolgathering. By the end of the period they had her pressed up against the windowsill playing with the venetian blind cord and not knowing what was happening to her.

I'd love to write a book for children on how to improve the behavior of their teachers and parents. (Give them what they want in return for what you want.) Or would that be seditious? Positive reinforcement is so easy to learn and so frighteningly powerful.

Body Contact

There's something about touching that I don't quite understand. Why should a handshake be so universally satisfying? Why are we drawn to a shaker who touches

145

our upper arm with his left hand? Why when someone is really devastated does a hug or an embrace ease the pain?

I remember our three-year-old getting rammy and kicking his toys a bit. "Hey, Rich, what's the matter? Do you need a hug?"

"Yeah," and he'd come over and I'd pick him up and pat him on the back for half a minute. Then he'd slither down and be off again, batteries charged.

Some time ago I was walking down the hallway past some church classrooms. Standing outside of one was the ten-year-old terror of Sunday School teachers, with head hung down and shoulders slumped.

"What's the matter, Ken?"

"Nothin'."

"Tough time in class?"

"Yeah."

"You look like you need a hug." I walked over, put my arms around his shoulders, and patted him gently on the back. In a few moments he put his arms around my waist. It didn't last more that thirty seconds.

"Well," I said, extracting myself, "I hope the rest of your day is better."

"Yeah . . . Thanks."

The next week I was in the same building in the foyer. There were people all around and I was busy.

"How's your committee doing?" I asked one.

"Regards to your family," to another.

"See you Thursday night."

And there was ten-year-old Kenny, standing on the

edges, watching me. As soon as there was a break, he walked up and said, "You look like you need a hug."

"Yes," I laughed, "I sure do." We hugged for about half a minute, and then he was gone.

The following week it was the same scene, except that he didn't wait for a break. He just came up and hugged me, patting me on the back. I patted him on the back while I continued talking to an adult, "I'll have those reports by the end of the week."

I had the feeling they were the only hugs he got all week. They were important to him.

Incidentally, Kenny was classified as emotionally disturbed in the public schools, and a teacher's aide in his class of eight was assigned to stay by his elbow to control him when he would punch out other children.

Soon after this he was involved for six weeks in a foster family setting. The principal of his new school didn't have his records and placed him in a regular fifth grade. Can you predict what happened?

Yes, he got into trouble the second day. He failed to complete his homework and had to stay after school! But other than that, he was a bright, normal kid, living in a stable home environment with rules, chores, and hugs.

Six weeks later he was back home, where he upset his parents and punched out other "emotionally disturbed" kids.

Don't misunderstand me. Hugs may have helped, but the key was that his environments expected different things of him.

Touches, hugs, and pats can be very reinforcing. But Anglo-Americans find it difficult to show love and approval physically, even though their children need it. Mediterranean, African, and Latin cultures are much more spontaneous in using this powerful tool. Anglos would do well to watch and learn.

A caution to teachers: as beautifully as children respond to touch and as badly as you may want to encourage them by hugs or pats, you'll do well to keep your hands off. Someday in your school some kid is going to say, "Mr. Nelson fondled me."

If you've never touched a student, at least you'll have the moral advantage of truth. But if you've been a toucher you'll always wonder if you might have been misunderstood and brought the whole affair down around your head. Not that truth will matter in public. Your career is finished. You'll always be known as "Wasn't he the teacher who was accused of. . . ?" Move to another state, get a job selling pipe valves and try to forget.

But enough of that. This is a happy chapter.

Primary Positive Reforcers

Primary reinforcers are what the child really wants. They can be anything he/she likes in the way of treats, things, activities, or privileges.

We don't know what they may be. It's been a long time since we were children, or maybe the world in which we grew up was different. The only way we can be sure is to ask the children.

"Hey, kids, come sit with me for a minute and help

me. I'm making a list of things that you like to have or do and I'm not sure where to start."

You'll hear a wide variety, many of which you'd never considered as rewarding.

"Desserts. I like desserts." You write down, "Extra dessert if there is one."

"A new back pack."

"New back pack," you write.

"I like to go to the movies."

"Movies, parents' choice," you add.

"Milkshakes."

"New bike. I need a new bike."

"Wait a minute," you counter. "We're on a budget. How about some things that don't cost anything?"

"I like to have friends stay overnight."

"Walks in the woods."

"Extra reading time before lights out."

"Rides to the mall."

"Pennies to take to Gurk's for candy."

"Sleep with Mom 'til Daddy comes home."

At school, primary reinforcers are oriented to the classroom.

"New pencils."

"New tablets."

"Choose our own seats for the day."

"Extra ten minutes recess."

"NFL football book covers"

"Sit on the rug in the back and read magazines."

You write, "Sit quietly on the rug in the back and read magazines after other work is done."

"Get out of homework one night."

"Oh," you offer, "but homework is not a punishment so not doing it can't be a reward." Or, more wisely, you can just quietly leave that off the list you're compiling.

At work, primary positive reinforcers include a plaque with the engraved names of "Employee of the Month," and perhaps a picture in the monthly newsletter.

A special parking place, close to the entrance.

A carpet on the floor and your name on the door.

The key to the executive washroom.

My father-in-law was a top insurance salesman. His kitchen was filled with blenders, waffle-irons, and juicers. There were trips to Hawaii and the Carribean.

Mary Kaye's top salespeople drive themselves first and pink Cadillac convertibles later. Now, that wouldn't move me at all. Offer me a pink convertible and I'll sit on my hands. It would even be punishing for me to have to drive a pink convertible into my regular service station. But a long dark green Jaguar sedan, ah, now that's motivating.

Primary reinforcers are the real thing, what we really want and what we're willing to work for. They're different for different people. We can add some we think the kids will like, but we can't assume we know.

(The purists among us will argue that the real primary reinforcers are the validation, attention and prestige that pink Cadillacs represent, and that all the rest are secondary reinforcers. Well, okay, but for our purposes—rough and dirty—let's stick with the way we've got it outlined here.)

Secondary Reinforcers

Secondary reinforcers are things that represent primary reinforcers—as we're using the term. They make it convenient to reward people close to the time of their behavior. They give people freedom to choose their own primary reinforcers.

For example, what I really want is a roof over my head and groceries in the cupboard. It's too complicated for my employer to provide these things, so I'm given secondary reinforcers (dollars) so that I can trade them in for what I really want. I will work just as hard for the secondary reinforcers as I would for the primary ones.

But there are other primary reinforcers that are hard to pinpoint. I would like a little respect and dignity. How do you get that from your employer?

Well, he can give you secondary reinforcers (dollars) which you can then trade in for long dark green Jaguar sedans, and then when you drive by people will say, "Wow, what a fine car. The fellow who owns that must be really valued by his employer to be paid enough by buy that."

Reb Tevya put it best: "When you're rich, they think you really know."

Or, in my business, you can be promoted to the rank of full professsor. That gets me the grand sum of $200 more per year, but people think, "Wow, he's a full professor. The administration must really admire his services to promote him to such etherial ranks."

There are lots of different kinds of secondary

reinforcers. Jim Carey in "The Mask" does a spoof on a stage star gushing over an audience's applause: "You love me! You *really* love me!" You can use applause, praise, certificates of appreciation, sweater letters, pins, stars on a chart, decals, pogs, tokens, or whatever as secondary reinforcers.

Stars

My children used to earn stars from their grade school teachers for reading library books. Stars on a chart are especially good for children who want their names and accomplishments to be seen by others.

I once had a student who was an assistant coach for the Philadelphia *Eagles*. During his tenure they kept a four by eight feet sheet of plywood over the door of the locker room, with all the players' names painted on it. He put bright red circular tags next to the names of team members who had made especially good plays during the last game. He was amazed at how important that was to them. It was the first thing they looked at the day after a game.

Another student coached midget football among early adolescents. They earned little stickers for their helmets for really hustling or for especially good plays. They loved it and played their little hearts out to earn them.

The Boys Scouts and Cubs understand the principle. Cubs earn wooden beads and all sorts of knicknacks for their uniforms. Scouts earn patches and pins for their hard work. Does the boy really want to study "Citizenship in the Community"? No. What he really wants is that cool merit badge patch (a secondary reinforcer), and if he gets enough of them he'll be elevated to Eagle Scout and lots of people will come to his Court of Honor and he'll get his picture in the paper and he'll get dignity and respect all his life. (That's true, too. I've often heard comments from mature men—professionals and executives—that so-and-so was an Eagle Scout.)

Boys recognize, however, that in some circles being a Scout does not bring respect. They love the patches at camp, but wouldn't be caught dead in their uniforms at school. Sad.

Points

Some teachers, also, have realized that secondary reinforcers such as stars even can be punishing if they're shown in public. Further, the lack of stars may be too discouraging to a child whose skill levels will never equal his peers. So they've switched to giving points, kept on a chart by the teacher.

Some years ago a naval officer retired and finished his degree in psychology. He was particularly taken by the success of behavior modification techniques as taught by B. F. Skinner. This former officer opened a special school for emotionally disturbed (read: discipline problem) children to which the local school districts could send their unmanageables. He was extraordinarily successful.

Unfortunately, after a few years he retired from that as well. Now the school uses standard points for standard behaviors, logged on clipboards by aides and cashed in once a week for money. Although the school has expanded, the joy has gone out of the program. I want to show you how to avoid that.

Token Economy

I mentioned under "Negative Reinforcement" a reformatory in Maryland that had been suffering from a 70% recidivism. That is, 70% of the youths who completed their sentences were rearrested and returned to the facility. Obviously, the institution was ineffective.

They introduced *a behavior modification program using positive reinforcement through a token economy.* Now, that's a mouthful, but it says it all.

They decided that instead of simply punishing the kids, they would concentrate on modifying their behavior to be acceptable to the community.

The principle they would use in this behavior modification would be positive reinforcement, which, loosely speaking, is a reward system.

The technique of positive reinforcement would be a token economy.

A token economy avoids the public display of rewards, such as you get with stars and badges which can be ridiculed by the "ten percenters."

A token economy avoids the horrendous bookkeeping problem placed on aides, as you have with points on a chart. It also gives the child a constant update on his progress, which he doesn't have when the aide has the clipboard.

In this token economy, the child got only the very basics. He got a bed, some standard issue underwear, a gray shirt and gray paints. He was given this without his having to lift a finger.

Petey at the pool table: "Say, I'll play the winner."

"It costs a token to play," an aide informs him.

"Token? Where do you get tokens?"

"It depends. Sometimes you get them in class. Sometimes at bed check. Sometimes at morning inspection. It varies."

"Class? I ain't never goin' to class."

"Suit yourself."

Pretty soon the child sees that some of the other kids live pretty well. They've got regular street clothes, they have access to recreational equipment, they have furniture in their rooms and many of the good things in life. They buy or rent them with tokens.

The next morning an aide approaches Petey. "Nice job on your bed this morning. The blankets are straight and the pillow's been plumped up. I think you ought to have a token."

Petey spends it immediately on a half hour at the pool table. Everybody else is in class.

The next day there's more praise over the made bed and another token. Petey saves it to play with the other guys after class. Bored, he walks by a classroom and looks in.

The teacher sees him and calls out, "You're Pete,

aren't you? I'm glad you came to class. Here's a token. You can sit over there."

Within a few days, Petey has earned tokens for coming to class, remembering his book, taking notes, asking a good question, and not muttering under his breath in class as much as he had been.

After a couple of weeks he has spent tokens to get regular clothes, a bedside table and lamp, shaving foam and deodorant, and back issues of magazines.

He has begun to learn that his actions have consequences, and that is a very healthy concept.

But there are a lot of people out there who resist token economies. The usual criticisms include the following:

- "You're going to have to wait a long time before you can reward some kids,"
- "Who's going to run around behind them the rest of their lives giving them tokens?" and
- "You're just bribing them."

Not to worry. We'll address each of these shortly.

The beautiful thing about the token economy at the Maryland reformatory is that their recidivism completely reversed. Instead of 70% being rearrested and coming back, only 30% did so. Show me another system that changes critical behavior by 40%. This works.

I once worked with a school system that had four sixth grades: 6A, 6B, 6C, and 6D. "D" for dregs. "D" for disaster. "D" for discipline problems.

Ask any elementary school teacher how many students make up the ideal class. The answer is "Three less than I have now if I get to choose the three."

This school had decided to take the troublemakers out of the other three classes and lump them all together into 6D. That way as the students moved as a body from one subject room to another the teachers would have three pleasant classes and only one bad one.

And they were bad. They'd come pushing and shoving into the room, cursing and shouting at each other and baiting the teacher. They called each other nigger and honkey and Big Ears and Dork. One little girl had taken up residence in the trash can at the back. Freud would have had fun with that, or was it just the influence of Sesame Street?

Some teachers just tried to endure. The science teacher planned entertainment—bicarbonate of soda and vinegar volcanoes, erosion pans, anything to get through forty minutes. The health teacher used bombast to try to cower them. In desperation some of the teachers cried for help.

We talked with the five teachers and got the cooperation of four. The health teacher didn't want any part of bribing kids to do what they're supposed to do anyway.

The pupils of 6D (I can't call them students) heard something like this:

"We'd like to give you some of the things you like, and you can get them by doing some of the things we like. Is that fair? [Kids love "fair."] There's no budget, so they can't be things we'll have to buy. What kinds of privileges or special activities do you like?"

We got what you might expect—extra minutes of

recess, choose seats, time with the magazines in the back, library passes, etc. We added a few others we thought they'd like, such as sitting at the teacher's desk, and keeping the attendance log. Eighteen of these nineteen terrors agreed to try this. That was Wednesday.

After school we sat together and decided on prices for different "cash-ins," as we called them. Some were cheap—one token, to provide for immediate reinforcement. Others which were inconvenient to the teacher, such as extra recess time, were more expensive. One or two outrageous requests were priced out of the market.

We'd gotten a batch of several hundred plastic tokens about the size of dimes from a Bingo facility. The teachers armed themselves with a few dozen in their pockets.

Thursday was incredible. I'm reluctant to describe it because it seems not possible. These were *bad* kids. But on Thursday 6D moved from room to room in order. They came in and sat in their assigned seats. They had their books and they sat expectantly with open notepads.

The teachers were dumbfounded. The kids were getting tokens like salted peanuts. But the teachers actually were able to teach a lesson, something some of them never quite had been able to do with this group. The children were enthusiatic. Even the one holdout asked if he could join after a couple of days.

Now, watch what happened. Since they were getting tokens for being attentive, they actually began to succeed on quizzes. One girl cried when she got a perfect score and after school ran home with her paper.

At the end of the marking period one boy had earned—earned, mind you—a place on the honor roll.

The science teacher had a unit on optics. Everyone traced, cut out, and taped up his own pinhole camera, then braced against something outside and exposed his film for five seconds. Guess who was the first sixth grader—from 6A, 6B, 6C, and 6D—to develop and print the first picture in the closet darkroom? Trashcan Sally.

The kids stopped hassling each other. Somebody noticed "Big Ears" drawing race cars, and everyone gathered around and thought that he drew better than Ryan in 6B. After that they dropped the nickname.

Syreene and Tommy Wayne cashed in tokens for extra recess at the same time. They ended up playing jacks together on the steps outside the classroom. A local police officer came by and saw them.

He sneered at the boy, "What are you doing? Jacks!? What are you, some kind of pansy?"

"Uhhhh," the teacher groaned when he heard this. "Don't worry about it," the boy answered. "What's he know, anyway."

Other classes began lobbying for a token economy, and 6D became the favorite class of all the teachers, except the health teacher, who called them mercenaries. True story. I saw it happen.

Nathan Azrim, co-author with R.M. Foxx of "Toilet Training in Less than a Day," gives an early example of a token economy introduced in a closed ward of a psychiatric hospital. These were twenty-one hopelessly schizophrenic women with no prospect of ever being released.

First he introduced them to some pleasures. For example, there might be 4:00 o'clock walks around the grounds, movies in the day room, a rocking chair by the window, a private cubicle with bedside table and lamp, and similar niceties.

After a week or so, he announced that from now on, if the patients wanted these things they'd have to buy them.

"We don't have any money. How can we buy them?"

"Oh, money's no good here. You'll use tokens."

"How do we get tokens?"

"By behaving as people do in the outside community. And that may be a little different for each of you. Ursa, you can get tokens by not screaming out the window at passersby. Verna, you can get tokens by not talking so much. Wilma, you'll get tokens by talking more. Xyla, we'd like to hear less about the CIA's radio implant behind your ear. Zarah, you'll earn tokens by not hitting other people.

Using the principles of shaping and thinning, which we'll talk about shortly, Azrin was able to change the psychotic behavior of these girls to the point where half of them were released into the community by the end of a year.

Were they cured? Well, we don't know. Probably not. But the behavior that had gotten them committed was changed, and that's what was needed to get them into a less restrictive environment.

Oh, they weren't executive secretaries making 30K per year. They were doing things like clerking at the local five-and-ten, or living in a half-way house at night and helping a landscaper during the day, or serving as a companion for an old lady, living with her, shopping for her and watching television with her.

I've seen films of mildly and moderately retarded children learning things their parents never dreamed they'd be able to do. The primary reinforcers were love and attention, and the secondary reinforcers were treats and tokens.

Behavior modification through positive reinforcement using a token economy has worked well with prisoners, psychotics, recalcitrants, and retardates. But what about normal children in normal homes?

Here is where the token economy really shines, for not only does it improve behavior but it improves the quality of life at home. It teaches children responsibility, it offers them freedom, and it allows parents to enjoy doing nice things for their children. Bickering and criticism stops and the home becomes a haven for all who live there. Does this sound like it's worth a try to you?

But there are some pitfalls. There are some things you need to understand before you try it, or you will fail and not know why. Let's spend a few minutes in a crash course in psychological conditioning so that when you install your token economy you'll have the overnight success that's possible.

Shaping

Suppose you want your child to overcome his awful table manners. You'll wait a long time if you wait for him to show banquet behavior before you reward him. You're going to have to settle for what you can get at first.

"Arnie, you were looking at your fork! I'll bet you were thinking that someday soon you're going to start using a fork. That's wonderful. I think you ought to have a token for thinking about improving your table manners."

Is Arnie going to protest that he wasn't thinking anything about table manners and that you ought to keep the token? No, he wants the token because it can help buy him something he wants.

Will he look at his fork again? Yes, and you'll smile and nod, and say, "Good boy."

Hmmn. No token that time.

Arnie pushes his fork out of the way to get to the peas that fell off his spoon. "Arnie, you touched your fork! That's great. You'll be eating like a grown-up soon and we'll be able to take you out in public. Here's another token."

Gradually, slowly, you reinforce his "successive approximations of the desired behavior." This is called *shaping*.

Oh, I can hear the protests echoing from the 1960's, "You're manipulating the child!"

Yes, we're manipulating the child just as Michelangelo manipulated marble, and for the same worthy purpose. Neither unsculpted marble nor untrained kids are much fun to be with.

B.F. Skinner tells of shaping pigeons to peck a white dot on the side of their cage. Attached to the cage is a little cup, and the cup is attached to a tube leading to an elevated hopper full of corn. Whenever Skinner wants, he pushes a button and a grain of corn drops into the cup. (When rigged to be automatic, this is the well-known "Skinner box.")

The psychologist watches the pigeon as it wanders around the cage. Whenever it approaches the white dot, he presses the button and a kernel of corn appears in the cup. The pigeon pecks it up.

After a few aimless strolls around the cage, sometimes coming near the white dot, the pigeon knows that for some reason he's getting corn. You can almost see his little bird brain trying to figure out what he's doing that's causing the corn to appear. It's only minutes before he decides that being close to the white dot has a corn-producing effect, and he trots back and forth between the dot and the cup.

Then Skinner requires a little more. The pigeon needs to look at the white dot, his head in proximity to it, before it gets reinforced. This is quickly mastered.

Next he requires an actual peck at the dot, but if that's what this psychologist wants, that's what the pigeon will give him. The pigeon's behavior has been *shaped* and he has been conditioned to peck white dots.

Skinner carried this to extremes. He's taught pigeons to do all kinds of strange things, such as playing pigeon ping-pong with the table at neck level and the pigeons getting reinforced only when they get the ball past their pigeon opponent.

During WorldWar II the Allies had missile capabilities but lacked electronic guidance systems. Skinner conditioned pigeons to peck at a dot on a screen. The dot corresponded to the aim of a missile. When the inertial system sensed the missile was moving off course, the location of the dot on the screen would change. The pigeon would peck on it, and the course would be corrected. When it finally hit the target, BLAMB, feathers and all.

The powers that be in the new Pentagon building nodded and smiled at this crackpot professor from Harvard, humored him and sent him home.

Some entrepreneurs on the old Steel Pier in Atlantic City used to have a series of glass cages, each with a single chicken living in it.. If you put a dime in the slot, music would play and the chicken would perform a little dance. When the music stopped, you walked away marveling at these intelligent chickens. What you didn't notice was that when the music stopped the chicken went immediately to a little cup to collect his kernel of corn. The stupid chicken didn't realize that the corn dropped automatically whether he danced or not. He'd been conditioned to dance at the music to earn the corn.

A more humiliating display had a chicken that would play tic-tac-toe with you for a quarter, and the chicken almost always won. You'd walk away worrying about brilliant chickens who were going to take over the world.

(You know, don't you, that there is a sequence which almost guarantees winning at tic-tac-toe?)

Today we have porpoises carrying hooks to the bottom of the ocean and snagging used second-stage rocket casings, saving the taxpayers millions of dollars. Skinner was ahead of his time.

It used to be that moviemakers had to tame wild animals and then train them to do tricks on-camera. Today they skip the taming part and simply shape the animals to perform by rewarding them for increasingly complex tasks. If you remember Disney's "Charlie, the Lonesome Cougar," you were watching an untamed animal. It was the cameraman who was in the cage, for his own protection.

Thinning, or Fading, Reinforcers

In a legitimate question about token economies, some critics ask, "Who is going to be around to reinforce these children with tokens the rest of their lives?" The answer simply is, "No one." If you get them on the proper schedule of reinforcement, it's not necessary.

Let's be sure that you understand this critical phase of establishing a token economy.

Schedules of Reinforcement

Some years ago while I was a student in college, the psychology department brought in B.F. Skinner, the grand high priest of psychology at the time. They planned to have him speak to different groups throughout the day, but some of us just followed him around and attended all the lectures, standing in doorways or sitting on the floor as necessary. I remember him as a mild and pleasant fellow, full of good humor, who didn't take himself too seriously.

I remember particularly his discussion of schedules of reinforcement. Schedules of reinforcement have to do with how often the subject is rewarded and how much he gets. My notes from that day tell the following story.

Constant Reinforcement
Extinguishes Quickly

Skinner had set up his "Skinner box," that is, a pigeon cage with a white dot and a cup to receive grains of corn for the pigeon. Using shaping, he soon had the pigeon conditioned to peck the white dot in order to get a grain of corn dropped into his cup.

The pigeon was on a constant *interval* schedule. That is, each and every time he pecked the white dot he got a grain of corn. The bird was also on a constant *ratio* schedule. That is, he got one grain and only one grain each time he pecked.

Then, that's it, pigeon. No more corn. Peck all you like, but no corn will drop into the cup. He was cut off from his reinforcement.

How long will the pigeon continue to peck vainly at the white dot?

Peck. No corn.

Peck again. No corn.

Peck a third time. Still no corn.
Walk around the cage a bit. Come back and peck.
No corn.
Peck again. No corn.
Walk around some more. Back for another try.
Still no corn.

The average pigeon in this experiment, trained under a schedule of constant reinforcement (that is, he had always gotten one grain for one peck), continued to peck the white dot thirteen more pecks after the corn stopped coming. That's not very much.

If we extrapolate to people (sometimes a very iffy thing to do), and we assume that you have conditioned your child to make his bed and to expect one token each and every time he does, then we may predict that after two weeks in his/her own apartment, bedmaking behavior will become extinguished because you're not there doling out the tokens. That's not very satisfying if you're trying to prepare a child to be independent.

Or, suppose you eat at the same beanery every lunch time. Your waitress is pleasant, and you leave a 15% tip every day. We may expect the quality of your service to become rather matter-of-fact as she begins to take you for granted. She serves, you tip. No big deal.

Try another. You have a job that pays you every two weeks—a constant interval. You get the same salary no matter what—a constant ratio of reinforcement. No matter how hard you work, how many hours you put in, nor how successful you are at what you do—every two weeks the same check. If money is your reinforcer, this is almost guaranteed to create in you a matter-of-fact, lackluster performance.

Does this sound like your job? Think of what it does to school teachers, and you may have discovered what is wrong with American education.

Variable Ratio And Interval Lasts

Part Two of Skinner and the Pigeons. Dr. Skinner went on to describe what happened when, having gotten the pigeons conditioned to peck the white dot by using a schedule of constant reinforcement, he began to *thin*, or *fade*, the reinforcement.

Peck the white dot. Get a grain of corn.

Peck again. No corn.

Peck again. No corn.

Peck again. Ah, there's a grain.

Peck again. No corn.

Again, and again, and again. Nothing.

Peck again. One grain. Ah!

Peck six times before another reinforcement.

Peck three times before a grain drops down.

Peck ten times.

Then twice.

Then seven times.

The poor pigeon never knows when he'll be reinforced, and he keeps pecking away.

After some while under this schedule of variable reinforcement, at least a variable *interval* although the constant *ratio* (one grain) remained, Skinner turned off the corn entirely.

Will the pigeon peck more times after his last reinforcement or less times, as compared to pigeons conditioned with constant schedules?

Right! More times. How many more? Twice, or twenty-six pecks?

No, more than that.

Ten times more?

No, more than that.

Come on, now. A hundred times more?

Actually, the average pigeon goes for more than three thousand more pecks after his last reinforcement. We know it was more than three thousand because the experimenters got tired and shut the experiment down after that number.

Stupid pigeons. Well, what do you expect from a bird. But surely we're not suggesting that your child, a bright human being, would hang on so doggedly? Are we?

You've seen it happen.

"Mommy, can I have a cookie?"

"No, dear. It's too near dinner."

"Just one cookie, Mommy."

"No, dear, I told you it's too near dinnertime."

"I just want one. Only one. Please Mommy."

"How many times do I have to tell you? You'll ruin your appetite!"

"No, I won't. I want a cookie. I want a cookie. Cookie, cookie, cookie, I want a cookie."

"Oh, all right, just one."

You've got the child on a schedule of variable reinforcement. Next time she's going to bug you for three thousand more buggings before the bugging behavior is extinguished. Just one reinforcement after you've said "no" is almost guaranteed psychologically to condition your child to drive you out of your mind in whines.

Can adults be conditioned? Consider the finest Skinner boxes in the world, manufactured by the high-tech Bally Corporation. You can watch them in action in Atlantic City, Las Vegas, and a few other places around the country.

You stand shoulder to shoulder with hundreds of other people in the room. You put your quarter in. You pull the lever. Sometimes—not always—you get some quarters back. You are on a schedule of variable reinforcement—a variable interval (times) and a variable ratio (amount).

It works like this. The people who run casinos are not gamblers. You may have the image of the president of the Showboat Casino as being a riverboat character with white suit, broad hat and slim cigar. Or maybe you've pictured the CEO of the Golden Nugget as being a Humphrey Bogart type straight out of Casablana. No, no. I know these people. They are conservative businessmen, lawyers and accountants, in Brooks Brothers' suits with children in school and wives who volunteer at the hospital.

They know exactly how much will be paid out per dollar put in. Typically it's about 85% paid back. That is, for every $100 you drop into a slot machine, the machine is programmed to give back $85.

If it gives back less than 85%, they send out a fellow to fix it, because they know you'll become discouraged and quit at less than that amount. If it gives back more than the pre-set percentage, the repairman goes out in a hurry, because these are businessmen who know how much profit they need to pay their bills.

The slot machine pays back on a variable schedule. You never know when nor how much. And if you give up too soon, the next person on that machine will get what you didn't.

Your service club sponsors a bus trip to the casinos. "No," you tell them, "I don't gamble."

"That's okay," they say. "Support the club by coming with us. You can go up on the boardwalk and watch the waves and feed the pigeons.

Well, all right.

When you arrive at the casino, a pretty girl gets on the bus and welcomes everyone.

"We're glad you're with us today, and to help you get in the spirit of the fun, here's a roll of forty quarters to start with."

"Oh, no thanks," you protest. "I don't gamble. I'm just along for the ride."

"That's fine," she says. "We're glad you're here and we want you to enjoy yourself. Take the roll and have some fun. We're in the recreation industry."

Well, it's not really gambling if you're using their money, is it? I mean, they expect you to put it in the machines. It wouldn't be right if you kept it, or spent it on food or salt water taffy for yourself, would it? The best thing to do is just go in and lose it all, and then go out on the boardwalk.

Now, you've got forty quarters to lose. You don't know it, but your machine is designed to give you back 85% per cent of what you put in.

That is, you put in some quarters, but a few come back. You put them in also, but some come back. You never know when and you never know how many. You're on a schedule of variable reinforcement.

Mathematically, it goes something like this.

You put in 40 quarters. You'll get 85% of them back, or 34. What do you do with them?

You put in the 34. You get back 29.

You put the 29 in. You "win" 25.

You put in the 25. 21 come back.

You stand there and insert the 21. Still, you get 18.

Put the 18 in. 15 return.

You play 15. 13 come back.

The 13 win you 11.

11 get you 9.

9 get 8 returned.

8 brings 7.

Then 6, 5, 4, 3, 2, 1, and finally, they're all gone.

In trying to get rid of your 40-quarter roll, how many times have you put a quarter into the slot machine?

Typically, 251 times, all on a powerful schedule of variable interval and variable ratio.

"Uh, that was, uh, fun. Look, I feel lucky. Uh, don't worry about me, I'm going to buy another roll of quarters and I'll see you back on the bus."

You are now conditioned, just like the pigeon with

the white dot. And you will pull and pull for three thousand more pulls, or until the money you saved out for the phone bill and the dentist is gone.

Preference For Variable Interval

We're talking about using tokens in conditioning the behavior of children. There's every indication that after you've got the child conditioned on a constant schedule, you should thin to a variable schedule.

But I have found that thinning the *interval*—how often the child is reinforced—is effective enough. I believe making a variable of the *ratio*—the number of tokens the child gets—just complicates the effort and isn't necessary. I can see how it might even be counterproductive as you get involved with how many tokens you should give for what kinds of behavior.

The school for emotionally disturbed children I mentioned earlier is into variable ratios. Three points for coming to class, one more point for bringing your book, two points for turning in a homework assignment, and so on. It can become an accounting nightmare, and we want to simplify your life, not complicate it. I suggest you stay with one token per reinforcement.

And in spite of the simplicity, this works.

Students in my class who choose to try a token economy at home use the following guidlines. Over the years we've refined it as we found that some techniques work better than others. What you have below is a distillation of the experiences of hundreds of parents, all boiled down to the last succulant drop.

Guidelines for a Token Economy

1. Determine what is rewarding to the child—ask him/her.

   a. Sit down with him and write up a list.

   b. Concentrate on activities and privileges rather than material items. Don't include money.

2. Then, by yourself or with your spouse, assign token values for each reward according to your interests.

   a. Be sure there are some low enough to provide immediate reinforcement, especially for younger children who cannot save.

   b. Carefully phrase or price the inconvenient ones high so that you don't have to pay out too often.

3. Explain the procedure to the child:

   a. You want him to have the things he wants.

   b. He can get them by doing some of the things you want.

   c. When he does, sometimes (not always) you will give him a token. [This provides intermittant—variable—reinforcement, which is very powerful.]

   d. If he asks for a token, you can't give him one.

   e. No subcontracting with other children.

4. Get tokens. Bingo chips are fine. Try exotic colors. Avoid using money as tokens.

5. Catch the child doing something good. Try your best to ignore those things you don't want him to do.

6. Give many tokens at first, laced with lots of sincere praise.

    a. Give tokens even for faint approximations of the ultimately desired behavior. (This is called "shaping.")

7. Allow immediate cash-ins, especially for small children. Go through the ritual of giving the token, then exchanging it for the reward.

8. Gradually thin the giving of tokens, but continue with the praise. (This is called "thinning," or "fading.")

9. Gradually thin the praise, but acknowledge with quiet thanks or smiles.

10. Reinforce often with praise, less often with tokens.

11. Never "fine" a child. He earned the tokens he has, and besides, the fining procedure may be rewarding because of the attention.

12. Ignore shocked relatives who complain you are bribing the child.

I suggest you follow these guidelines to the letter. There are subtle reasons for the wording in each item. I've tried to condense it down to the simplest words with all the bases carefully covered.

For example, suppose you decide to use dimes for tokens. Next week Uncle Bob comes to visit and the child shows off his collection of dimes. In his usual generous fashion, your brother gives him a five dollar bill, and the child thinks, "What a rip-off! I made my bed for a week for four measley dimes, and now I can get fifty by talking with my uncle."

In addition, you don't want the child to have fifty dimes and get his primary reinforcers for practically no effort. Worse, the child begins to equate good behavior with money, and he becomes mercenary. Don't use money. Follow the guidelines.

Phrase the cash-ins carefully. Instead of "Get ride to the mall—10 tokens," try "Get ride to the mall when convenient to Mom or Dad—10 tokens."

Set prices according to your own budget and pleasure. "Sleep over at a friend's house—3 tokens." "Have a friend sleep at our house—15 tokens." "Get a gas-powered trike—5280 tokens."

The Success of Token Economies

I recall teaching the concept in a Thursday class. When it met next on Monday, I noticed a rather outspoken student drumming her fingers on her desk waiting for class to begin. She looked steamed. Uh,oh. Trouble.

"Well," I began. Some of you said you were going to try a token economy at home. How did it go?"

Up shot her hand. "I have to tell you I'm really upset." She had everyone's attention.

"I've mentioned before I've had trouble with my ten year old for years. I've been through it all: teachers' conferences, child study teams, school psychologists, family counseling, juvenile authorities, everything. I started a token economy on Friday, and in one day he's made a complete turn-around! Why hasn't anyone shown me this before?"

Complete turn-around? "180°. He's all over the place doing things. He takes the laundry down when there's only a few things in it, loads the dishwasher without being asked. . .I can't keep up with all the things he's doing trying to earn tokens!"

We all should have such problems. And the best part about it is that his changed behavior lasted all through the semester, until I lost track of the family.

Another student had problems with a child who was a behavior problem at school. Now, it's a little much to try to convert a teacher to handing out tokens for you. But we found a solution.

Each day the parents gave the child a 3x5 card with each of his teachers' names on it. At the top was written, "If Todd did not disrupt your class today, please initial this card next to your name."

For each set of initials, Todd got a token when he got home.

If Todd knew he'd been disruptive, he didn't even

bother to ask the teacher for her initials. When he got home, his parents praised him and showed their pleasure for however many initials he'd gotten that day.

It would have been easy to berate him for only getting two today, but they remembered to ignore the poor behavior and reward the good.

The teachers were pleased at the parents' interest and Todd's improving behavior. But not understanding the principle, one kept refusing to initial the card and writing criticisms on it, because the boy was not quite perfect. Too bad. But it didn't matter much, because the parents ignored her criticism and praised what he had achieved. In a matter of *days*, Todd's long standing discipline problem evaporated.

Do you remember Donny, of the piano leaping and tattles from his classmates? His teacher set him up on tokens, which he could trade in at lunchtime and after school for M&M's. I'm not sure I agree with so much candy, because Donny made an about face and began earning handfuls of M&M's. He also began sitting in his seat, raising his hand instead of calling out, and actually doing well in his school work.

Then came the day when his teacher realized she was out of M&M's. "Donny, I'm so sorry! I meant to get some more last night but I forgot. Do you mind waiting until tomorrow?"

Here's a quote from Donny that warms my heart: "Aw, don't worry about it. I don't need 'em anymore."

Chapter 11—Criticisms of Token Economies: Do You Agree?

There have been a number of criticisms of token economies. I am not convinced any are valid. Most seem to come from people who've never tried it because they are philosophically opposed to the concept.

1. <u>Children should be good because they're supposed to be good.</u>

Yes, and it should never rain in Camelot. All the men should be brave, the women good looking, and all the children should be above average.

The fact is, children are by nature egocentric. Their brains have not matured to the point that they can conjure up much altruism. While we're waiting we can capitalize on that egocentrism by rewarding them for good behavior.

2. <u>You're just bribing them to be good, and that's manipulative and immoral.</u>

Yes, we're bribing them, just as your employer bribes you to come to work when you'd rather go to the beach. Are sales people manipulating customers when they sweeten the deal with premiums and discounts? I guess so, but it has an effect on my buying behavior, and I don't think that it's immoral.

3. <u>Children should feel our unconditional love regardless of their behavior.</u>

I'm still wrestling with this concept and I'm not sure how I'm going to resolve it. Should children have unconditional love? I think I could comfortably debate this either way.

On one hand I can argue—I do argue—that people deserve dignity and respect regardless of their behavior. A woman ought to stand by her man. Mother's should love their children and treat them tenderly, even when they're disobedient. A teacher should never humilate a student. An employer shouldn't criticize his staff in front of others. No child should go hungry.

I believe all this. I can't even fish and hunt, because I feel it's wrong to invade the animals' world for sport. But I keep a shotgun, and if my family were hungry I'd be among the first in the woods to harvest the deer. "Primitive" people have been known even to apologize and explain to a kill why thcy need its meat.

Sometimes children's behavior is a test. Children will test their parents' love by doing outrageous things. I believe we need to stand by our children even when they break our hearts.

I believe in unconditional love. I think.

Unconditional Love?

I remember an old story of two boys from prominent families in a small town. They got drunk and stole a car and wrecked it. Both families showed up to claim them at the police station. One had brought a suitcase and took their boy to the train station. The other family took their boy home and quietly endured the pain. I lean toward the latter.

"On the other hand. . ." Grandma used to say, "Beauty is as beauty does." That is, behavior is most important, regardless of the nature of the individual.

People do deserve dignity and respect, but I earnestly hope there's a special hell for the Ted Bundy's of this world. A woman ought to stand by her man unless he's an abusive brute who selfishly destroys her self-esteem. Mothers should love their children and treat them tenderly, but they've got to be careful not to let the children confuse love with approval. A teacher should never humilate a student, but teachers are human beings too and shouldn't have to endure hostility in their classrooms.

The patriot will argue that America was built on merit, not the accident of birth. The conservative says we must re-enthrone work as the ruling principle among our people. The theologian quotes, "If any would not work, neither should he eat."

The reactionary will go further. He will trace the decline of America from the day we decided that people have a *right* to public welfare, as compared to the public choosing to be compassionate and sharing their bounty. As long as we reward the idle with free rent, food, medical care, and schooling, we keep them as an underclass over whom we can feel superior. What we need is a little benign neglect. A few may suffer, but their suffering will stimulate thousands of others to get off the couch and learn the satisfaction of accomplishment in the face of struggle, as have generations before them. This is the secret of America's success, which we have forgotten.

Well, I believe that, too. I think.

This is all more philosophy than you bargained for, but the question is at the heart of child management.

I think I'm coming to believe that we show *real* love for children when we teach them that their actions have consequences. Good actions result in rewards, and poor actions don't. And that's one of the best arguments for a token economy.

Other criticisms come from people who don't quite understand the theory or mechanics. Let's look at some.

1. <u>We tried it and the kids drove us crazy asking how many tokens they would get, and refusing to do ordinary chores unless we promised them tokens</u>.

The answer is above, in "Guidelines for a Token Economy." If a child asks for a token, you're not allowed to give him one.

"Why not?" he complains.

A good answer is, "I don't know. That's what it says in the book." But actually, there are two answers. The one is that it keeps the child from bugging you to death. The other is that you're going to have to *thin* (or *fade*) the giving of tokens in order to get the child on a schedule of variable reinforcement. He won't like that much, but if he's not allowed to ask for one, it will keep you out of hassles.

2. <u>It worked okay for a while, but it lost its impact.</u>

It won't lose its impact if you are using primary reinforcers ("cash-ins) that the children really want. Check with the children again. Every child has his price. I think.

Or, perhaps the "cash-ins" are too delayed. "Seventy-five tokens and you can go to summer camp." That's a lot of secondary reinforcers (tokens) without a primary reinforcer (camp) to really condition the child.

You'll want to be sure you're giving out tokens frequently enough, to get the child conditioned. Maybe you thinned too quickly. You ought to be handing out six or eight tokens—laced with praise and attention— every day for the first couple of weeks.

There's a story here that boggles my mind. Our early guru, B.F. Skinner, was being interviewed by Elizabeth Hall, who at the time was editor of *Psychology Today.* He described a teacher somewhere in the Midwest who had worked out a "token economy" using little name slips. Whenever a child turned in a homework assignment or a project he/she got to put his name on a slip of paper and put it in a jar. On Friday afternoon, the jar was shaken up and a blindfolded classmate pulled the lucky name from the jar. So, the more homework done, the more chances to win a little prize which had been on display all week. The teacher chose the prize for the week, which included a hallowe'en costume, a small transistor radio, a tape of popular music, etc.

Can you see the fallacy here? I'm amazed that Skinner didn't. You've got thirty kids here wearing their little pencils down all week. How many get reinforced? One. How many work hard and don't get reinforced? Twenty-nine. That's awful!

It might work for a few weeks, but what happens when—through the luck of the draw—the kids see some sluggard win the prize? Or someone wins twice and many have never won? *That which is not reinforced tends not to be repeated.* The hard work behavior will become extinguished. I'm disappointed in Skinner.

On the other hand, many people continue playing the lottery without winning. Could it be that they're conditioned to enjoy the tension, the hope, the fantasy?

3. <u>My husband (wife, mother, etc.) wouldn't cooperate</u>.

Then, you stopped because you couldn't handle their disapproval, not because the technique doesn't work. At least try to persuade them not to interfere, then continue quietly on your own, trying not to use your token economy as a red flag in front of their bull. Remember, some people subconsciously *want* you to fail as a parent.

4. <u>What's to stop the children from stealing tokens</u>
   <u>from each other? Maybe we should use stars on</u>
   <u>a chart.</u>

Good question, and all I can say is that stealing
hasn't seemed to be a problem. I think I've figured out
why.

The tokens and even the "cash-ins" aren't really
what the children want. We use them and call them
secondary and primary reinforcers, but actually the true
primary reinforcer is the child's own feeling of self-
worth.

Consider a typical scene in school.

"Bertram, you're the worst student I've ever had!
You're irresponsible, thoughtless, and a troublemaker.
You'll probably be executed before you're thirty."

Bertram slumps in his seat and tries to pretend the
tirade doesn't bother him. His hands in his pockets, he
feels several small smooth disks. He takes them out and
lines them up on his desk.

"I got this one for making my bed without being
asked. This was for carrying down the laundry right
away. And this was for not arguing with Chris before
dinner. And, oh, yes, I stole these from Danielle."

No, that won't work. If the prime value of earning
tokens is to reinforce a child's self esteem in a world that
deprecates children, they won't work if they're stolen. I
think that's why we don't see much of it.

Does the possibility of their stealing still trouble
you? Then try using different colors for different
children. Bingo chips come in several different colors.

Stars on a chart? Again, some children are embarrassed by a public display of their fine achievements. And some are humiliated by their poor showing compared to the "Mommy's boy." But more than that, they can't take the stars with them as they can tokens and run them through their fingers and hold them up to the light and see the colors shining through.

Without tangible reinforcers in the form of tokens, they can't jingle them and relish the moments they received them, with accompanying hugs, praise, and smiles. There's nothing to prompt fantasies about what they'll do tomorrow to earn even more tokens, and the surprise on mother's face when they finally cash in an unprecedented twenty tokens and get to take their little friend to a matinee.

5. The little children lose the tokens, and I'm afraid they might choke on them.

Yes, the younger ones do lose them. Of course, that tells us what they really value. It's not the token, it's the approval and attention that came with it. So all is not lost when you find tokens left around the house. The child has still received what he wanted for his good behavior.

Choke on them? Yes, small children will eat anything. ("Eat anything?" the toddler counters. "You'd be amazed at how many things I have to try before I find something I can eat.") The answer, of course, is to choose for tokens something that's too big to choke on.

Try buying a set of big plastic poker chips at the Dollar Discount store, instead of the smaller bingo card covering disks we suggested above.

6. <u>My kids are too old for this.</u>

Hey, *I'm* not too old for this. Find what is truly reinforcing to me, and I'll do handstands for you. The primary reinforcers, the "cash-ins," are the key. Toddlers will cash in for "as-many-raisins-as-you-are-old." Middle children want "extra-dessert-if-there-is-one." Older children save to "have-a-friend-sleep-over." Young teens will collect tokens for "a-ride-to-the-mall-when-it's-convenient-for-Mom." Older teens will toe the line in order to get "the-family-car-for-Friday-night-if-it's-available."

I recall a teenager who had enjoyed the token economy as a child, but over several years the practice had lapsed in the family. Tokens did seem a little childish to her, but knowing she was an artsy-craftsy type, the parents tried little drops of colored glass, the kind used by stained glass artists.

I've heard of marriage counselors who have put their clients on a token economy, but I'm afraid to ask what they listed as "cash-ins."

There's an educational management company who hire themselves out to school districts who would like to try token economies in their schools. They go around to the local businesses and solicit prizes to be used as "cash-ins" for all ages of students. The businesses are delighted. They have a budget for community service, and if that can involve rewarding kids for achievement, that's great. And if it brings the kids and their families into their businesses, that's even better.

Elwood gets an 80% on his test. He gets a red card that he can cash in at McDonald's for a medium sized drink. Do you know how little that drink really costs McDonald's? Will Elwood buy anything to go with his drink? Will his parents, who brought him, buy anything or will they just sit and watch him? It's a win-win-win-win situation. Elwood's teacher is happy, Elwood is happy, McDonald's is happy, and the parents are happy. We should have more of this in the world.

Francesca gets a 90% on *her* test. She gets a gold card from her teacher. She can order a large burger, medium fries, and medium drink. Again, will she have anyone with her? Or, she can take her gold card to the sporting goods store and get 10% off her choice of athletic shoes. Win-win-win-win.

7. <u>Who is going to go around giving these kids tokens after they grow up?</u>

Ah, here we come to the crux of the matter, a criticism which often comes from otherwise competent psychologists. Again, I'm surprised and a little disappointed in them. They assume that it is the token or even the "cash-in" to which the child is conditioned.

They neglect the principle of *association*, those outcomes which are most closely associated with the behavior become the reinforcer.

For example, if you have antibuse in your bloodstream and you drink alcohol, you'll become nauseated. Soon you'll be conditioned to be nauseated when you drink alcohol even if you don't have antibuse in you.

Let's look at what happens when a child on a token economy makes his bed.

Child makes bed, feels good anticipating getting approval, praise, a token, and ultimately a "cash-in."

Each day he makes his bed and feels good while doing it as he anticipates all the reinforcement.

At first his parent gives him a token each day, lacing it with with attention and praise. He cashes in three tokens for an extra dessert one night, and another time three tokens for an extra half-hour of reading time before lights out.

This continues for a couple of weeks. But then his parent begins to thin the tokens. He doesn't get one every time he makes the bed, but he does get attention and praise. That's okay, and truth be told he'd probably even rather have the praise than the dessert.

Three or four weeks into the project, he's still making his bed and feeling good as he does so, anticipating the occasional smiles from his parent, less frequent praise, and even more rare tokens.

But what is most closely associated with the bed making? Cash-ins? No. Tokens? Rare. Praise. Not every day. Smiles and nods from parent? Sometimes. Feeling good? Yes!

Every day as he makes his bed he feels good, at first because of the reinforcement to come, but eventually because feeling good has become the conditioned result of bed making behavior.

Caregivers! I submit that when you have gotten your child to the point that he feels good when he does good, you have succeeded. You can have your life back, instead of spending it picking up after him or worrying that he's doing one dumb thing after another.

Your child is ready to be independent. You can send him out into the world and know that he's doing his homework. (We all have homework, all our lives, and the world belongs to those who do theirs.)

You can have some confidence that he won't be drinking and driving, because he's learned that his actions have consequences, like hurting other people or losing his license.

You'll have more confidence that your daughter won't be sleeping with every Don Juan with a smooth line and then showing up on your doorstep someday with a grandchild for you to raise. She knows that her future depends on her actions today. She learned it when she saved her tokens as a child.

Chapter 12—How to Keep Your Baby Quiet in Church

"Ba-ba-ba-ba-ba-ba! eeeeeeeEEEEEEEeeeeeee. No! NO! NOooooo. . ."

The woman on the pew in front of you turns with a look of mixed pity and distain. The teenager at the end of her row grins broadly. The bishop concentrates with sudden interest on the speaker, while his less experienced and less charitable counselor looks directly at you over his glasses.

It's time again. Time to gather the diaper bag and the bottle and the beads and the baby and join the exiles in the foyer. Goodbye, all. Goodbye. It's been nice being with you, all seventeen minutes of it. Excuse me. Excuse me, please. Excuse me for disturbing the meeting. Excuse me for being here, for wanting to see the speaker as well as hear him. Excuse me for wanting to be with the rest of my family and my friends, to rub shoulders with the saints and feel the spirit of the meeting.

What a paradox we church-goers face! Our children should be in church meetings. Brigham Young is quoted as saying he'd rather hear a child coo than an adult whisper. Yet we hear that crying babies, like promises, should be carried out immediately. And the "Foyer Branch" grows steadily larger and more irreverent every week. There are some out there who don't even try to come in to the meeting anymore. Rumor has it that the bishop is going to call a president, complete with counselors, clerk, and chorister.

Ah, but help is on the way. In three short weeks you're going to be settled in your meeting, with your family in order, reverent, attentive, and enjoying the spirit of the services. No longer will single adults shake their heads in disapproval. Grandmothers and missionaries with new members will vie for the privilege of sitting behind you. The bishop will smile benignly from the stand and you'll look up and down your pew with pleasure instead of chagrin.

The reason for this seeming miracle is that there are tricks to the trade of parenting just as vital and helpful as there are tricks to any trade—Making Rules that Stick, Negative Reinforcement, Positive Reinforcement. Sound familiar? They work at home, they work in the classroom, and they work in church. If you have better ways, by all means use them. But if yours don't create a pleasant, mild, loving, disciplined family during sacred meetings, then try these.

Positioning

Trick Number One: Positioning. You should consider a pew near the front. This keeps the children's visual field somewhat limited to the events on the stand instead of the whole fascinating sweep of the congregation. At least one pew in front of you restricts their territory and makes it easier to handle them than if they had the whole expanse of floor between the front bench and the podium.

Consider also placing your boys on one side and the girls on the other. The youngest should sit next to you on either side, with children of increasing ages toward the outside. This will put the ones who need most attention closest to you, and your older and more responsible children will be able to assist with middle children from the vantage of their end positions. The consistency of this arrangement will help them to settle down quickly each week. (Inconsistency breeds rule-testing and disruptive behavior.) The older ones will likely respond to your faith in them as you place them farthest from you. They'll appreciate the responsibility of helping the middle ones get through the meeting, and they'll be in the best position to help toddlers leave briefly for a bladder break.

Equipment

Trick Number Two: Equipment. You never saw a carpenter without tools. Why a parent?

First, be sure there are enough hymn books. Send older children to forage for them if there are not. Better yet, buy a couple extra ones to bring with you. (Order a different color from those the congregation uses so that you'll not have to cringe when you pass the music chairman on your way out.) During hymns, take a child's forefinger and move it across the notes like the bouncing ball of yesterday's movie sing-alongs. He'll enjoy the attention and action and incidentally come to grasp the concept of musical notation. Later, as attention spans weaken, the older children will turn to the hymn books for something to look at. I know children who play "Guess the Title" by calling out page numbers during long drives to meetings.

A pocket with a dozen or so three-by-five cards and a few stubby pencils will serve middle and older children well. There's not enough space to write letters and notes to friends, but it's sufficient for doodling, taking notes of talks, or illustrating talks by cartoons. By limiting books and elaborate toys you teach the principle that the meeting is really for listening and worshipping, not just a dull span of time to be endured any way possible.

Very small children for whom the talks are meaningless can be spared from utter boredom by a ration of "gimcracks" from your pocket. These are doled out one by one, each for a period of several minutes. An old one must be traded in for a new one, and the choice and time interval is yours, not the child's.

Successful gimcracks have included a small nut and bolt, paper clip, tiny plastic car, guitar pick, coiled spring, rubber band, cuff link, colorful button, cellophane tape spool, and just about any item with interesting shapes and texture. This procedure delights children and teaches them pleasure in small, simple things. It also helps them learn to tolerate periods of quiet inactivity, a necessary skill in life.

Conditioning

Trick Number Three: Conditioning. Were you aware that many children have been trained to misbehave in meetings? The parents don't know it, but they've done it as surely and successfully as if they'd planned it all beforehand.

This is how it happens. The singing is over, the sacrament trays are gone, and the deacons have joined their families. The bench is crowded and the child feels confined and bored. The air becomes warm and stuffy. Parent is inattentive to the child.

"Ba-ba-ba-ba-ba-ba."

"Shhhhhhh! Quiet! Be still!"

Well, at least that got some attention. Let's try some more. "eeeeeeeEEEEEEEeeeeeee."

"Shhhhhhh! Please be quiet. I want to stay and hear this talk."

But baby does not want to stay and hear this talk. "No! NO! NOooooo. . ."

Ah, here we go. Out to the cool carpeted foyer. Out to where they've got toys to play with on the floor, where there's room to crawl and other children to enjoy and hassle. Thank you, thank you. It took me a little while to understand that you required seventy-eight decibels before carrying me out. I'll give you that much earlier next week. And even louder, if that doesn't satisfy.

Dull, unpleasant environment. Disruptive behavior. Removal from unpleasant environment. You've used very effective negative reinforcement.

Disruptive behavior. Reward by being taken out to the pleasant foyer. You've used the even more effective positive reinforcement. Using both types you couldn't have planned a better method to teach poor behavior.

But just as children have been conditioned to be disruptive, they can be conditioned to be orderly. Here's how.

Modeling

The first technique is modeling. You should be a model of silence while in the meeting. No matter what the circumstances, do not talk. A quiet "shhhhh" or even a calm forefinger to the lips will convey your intent. Older children can write you a note and younger children can pantomime their most urgent needs.

Aversive Conditioning

The second technique is for older babes-in-arms: aversive conditioning. This requires a skilled hand and may take a little practice. With thumb and forefinger, search out the fleshy part on the back of the child's thigh. When he begins to babble, grip the thigh firmly and squeeze sharply. The trick is to inflict just enough pain to catch his attention but not enough to make him cry. When you see a look of shock and surprise cross his face you've done it hard enough, but then you must quickly gather him into a comforting position as you smother the whimpers with quiet "shhhhhh's" and soft humming. Be ready with another sharp squeeze, however, at the moment of the next disruptive outburst.

The above will extend your stay in the meeting for about fifteen more minutes. But finally the time will come when your comforting will not be sufficient and you'll have a full-fledged wail on your hands.

Carry the child out quickly. Walk right through the foyer, past his little playmates and far down the hall away from the congregation so they'll not hear what is yet to come. Carry him firmly and not especially gently. Let him know by your facial expression and tone of your voice that you're upset with him.

If you spank your children, this is a good time for a quick, sharp attention-getter on the soft padded part of the body. This may not be necessary—I know of highly successful parents who never spanked their children. But it does communicate your feelings quickly and motivates the behavior necessary to avoid repetition.

Continue to pace with the child in a dull, lonely part of the hallway. As he begins to quiet down, speak more kindly to him. When he is completely quiet, smile at him and reward him with hugs and comfort. Finally, ask him if he's ready to go back to the meeting. When he agrees, take him back cheerfully to rejoin your family in your regular pew.

The latter procedure, i.e., speaking kindly, hugging, and rejoining the interesting world when he conforms, you'll recognize as negative reinforcement.

Rewards to the Parent

The first week of this effort may require three or even four trips to the dreary hallway. Pay no attention to the stony stares from non-parents. If you follow the procedure faithfully, your baby will come to associate disruptive behavior with mild pain, disapproval, and banishment. On the other hand, he'll learn that quiet is rewarded with comforting body contact and the privilege of rejoining the land of the living.

And you, skilled parent, will be the envy of the congregation. You'll have an orderly and disciplined family, your meetings will be uplifting to you, and the Sabbath will be a delight for years yet to come, for you and your family, and for the members who will enjoy being with you.

Summary—A Last Word

Well, that's about it. I've taught you all I know. I have confidence that "Making Rules That Stick" —that is, consistency training—and "Discipline With a Smile," which is simple positive reinforcement using tokens, praise, and smiles, will change your life.

And more than that, I believe with B.F. Skinner and O.H. Mowrer that you don't need a degree in psychology to learn how to use these powerful tools.

The best psychologist is still a thoughtful intelligent mother. Don't be beaten down or manipulated by children. Use these proven techniques to bring them under control and you'll find that you can love them more than you used to. And your success will help you to love yourself as well.

Epilogue

OmniPress has other books in various stages of progress by the author and others writers of similar quality. If you would like to be alerted when a title comes off the press, write to OmniPress, Box 21, Sewell, New Jersey 08080.

<u>General Psychology</u>:

Family Bonding: How to Make Your Marriage Last All Your Life

Day-to-Day Psychology: Living with Other People

Dear Old Dad: Good Counsel for Good People*

<u>Children's Books</u>:

How to Fix an Unpleasant Teacher

A Swing Around the Solar System

Dear Old Dad Tells Bedtime Stories

Dear Old Dad Tells Scripture Stories

*"Dear Old Dad" is an advice column based in traditional family values. If your newspaper does not carry the column, you could encourage them to contact the OmniPress Syndicate at the address above.

Copies for Your Suffering Friends

If you have friends who are parents or teachers who might be interested in a copy of "Three Weeks to Better Kids" for themselves, why not just tear out one of the following pages for them? We'll get a copy out to them in twenty-four hours.

Epilogue

This book was composed entirely on a Macintosh computer using WordStar's WriteNow 4.0$^{®}$ word processing program. The text is 12 point Times and the headings are in Heather.

Here is some information on "Three Weeks to Better Kids" so you can order a copy for yourself or your stressed-out friends.

This 200-page book consists of two parts:

Part One, "Making Rules That Stick" teaches you consistency training.

Part Two, "Discipline with a Smile" explains the finer points of behavior modification through positive reinforcement.

Both techniques have been field tested by real live parents and teachers over a number of years. They work. They change lives. They're easy to apply, and they can even be fun.

The list price of the book is $19.95 each for one to four copies. More than four copies brings a 40% discount. For quantities of more than 500 for PTA's, school districts, social service or similar groups, call OmniPress at 1(800) 507-2272..08.

Send your check or money order for $19.95 now for twenty-four hour turnaround of your order. Add $3.00 if you'd like Priority Mail.

Your name_____
Address_____
Town_____State_____ZIP_____
Phone_(_____)_____
(In case we have a question on your order)

Make checks out to "OmniPress."

OmniPress
Box 21
Sewell, New Jersey 08080

Here is some information on "Three Weeks to Better Kids" so you can order a copy for yourself or your stressed-out friends.

This 200-page book consists of two parts:

Part One, "Making Rules That Stick" teaches you consistency training.

Part Two, "Discipline with a Smile" explains the finer points of behavior modification through positive reinforcement.

Both techniques have been field tested by real live parents and teachers over a number of years. They work. They change lives. They're easy to apply, and they can even be fun.

The list price of the book is $19.95 each for one to four copies. More than four copies brings a 40% discount. For quantities of more than 500 for PTA's, school districts, social service or similar groups, call OmniPress at 1(800) 507-2272..08.

Send your check or money order for $19.95 now for twenty-four hour turnaround of your order. Add $3.00 if you'd like Priority Mail.

Your name_____
Address_____
Town_____State_____ZIP_____
Phone_(_____)_____
(In case we have a question on your order)

Make checks out to "OmniPress."

Box 21
Sewell, New Jersey 08080

Here is some information on "Three Weeks to Better Kids" so you can order a copy for yourself or your stressed-out friends.

This 200-page book consists of two parts:

Part One, "Making Rules That Stick" teaches you consistency training.

Part Two, "Discipline with a Smile" explains the finer points of behavior modification through positive reinforcement.

Both techniques have been field tested by real live parents and teachers over a number of years. They work. They change lives. They're easy to apply, and they can even be fun.

The list price of the book is $19.95 each for one to four copies. More than four copies brings a 40% discount. For quantities of more than 500 for PTA's, school districts, social service or similar groups, call OmniPress at 1(800) 507-2272..08.

Send your check or money order for $19.95 now for twenty-four hour turnaround of your order. Add $3.00 if you'd like Priority Mail.

Your name_____

Address_____

Town_____State_____ZIP_____

Phone_(_____)_____

(In case we have a question on your order)

Make checks out to "OmniPress."

OmniPress
Box 21
Sewell, New Jersey 08080

Here is some information on "Three Weeks to Better Kids" so you can order a copy for yourself or your stressed-out friends.

This 200-page book consists of two parts:

Part One, "Making Rules That Stick" teaches you consistency training.

Part Two, "Discipline with a Smile" explains the finer points of behavior modification through positive reinforcement.

Both techniques have been field tested by real live parents and teachers over a number of years. They work. They change lives. They're easy to apply, and they can even be fun.

The list price of the book is $19.95 each for one to four copies. More than four copies brings a 40% discount. For quantities of more than 500 for PTA's, school districts, social service or similar groups, call OmniPress at 1(800) 507-2272..08.

Send your check or money order for $19.95 now for twenty-four hour turnaround of your order. Add $3.00 if you'd like Priority Mail.

Your name_____

Address_____

Town_____State_____ZIP_____

Phone_(_____)_____

(In case we have a question on your order)

Make checks out to "OmniPress."

OmniPress
Box 21
Sewell, New Jersey 08080